DAVID WEATHERLY

MONSTERS OF
THE LAST FRONTIER
CRYPTIDS & LEGENDS
OF
ALASKA
FOREWORD BY KEN GERHARD

Eerie Lights Publishing

DAVID WEATHERLY
MONSTERS OF
THE LAST FRONTIER
CRYPTIDS & LEGENDS
OF
ALASKA
FOREWORD BY KEN GERHARD
Based on interviews and research conducted by David Weatherly

ISBN: 978-1-945950-15-5 (Paperback)

Published by:

EERIE LIGHTS
Eerie Lights Publishing
eerielightspublishing.com

Cover design: Sam Shearon
www.mister-sam.com

Editor: A. Dale Triplett
@DaleTriplett

Book layout/design: SMAK
www.smakgraphics.com

Printed in the United States of America

Also by David Weatherly

Table of Contents

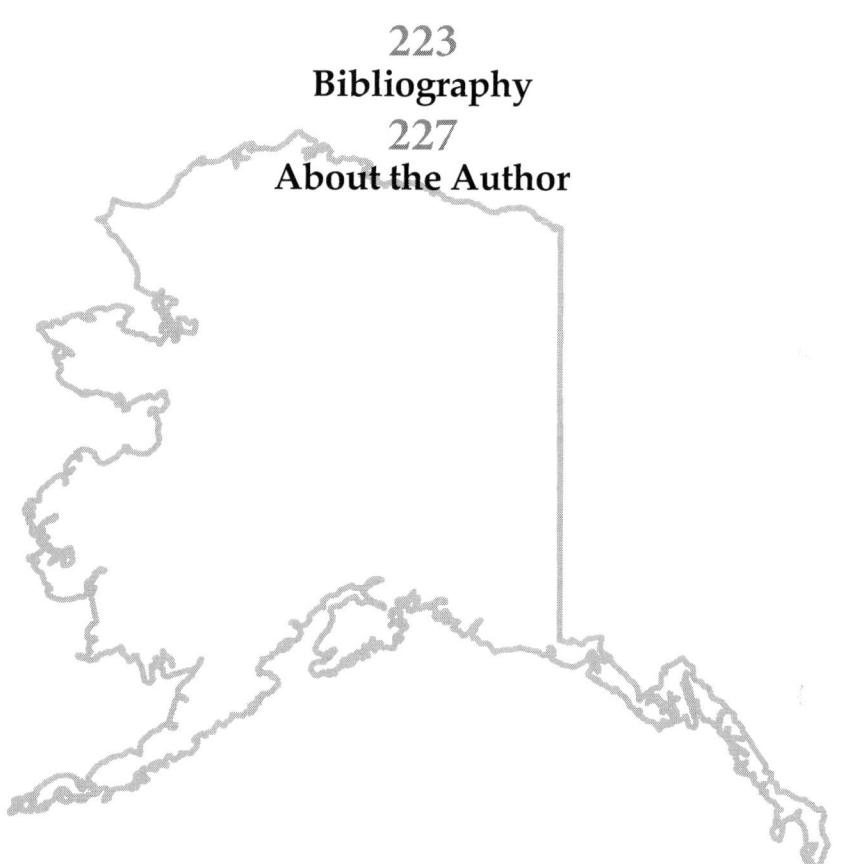

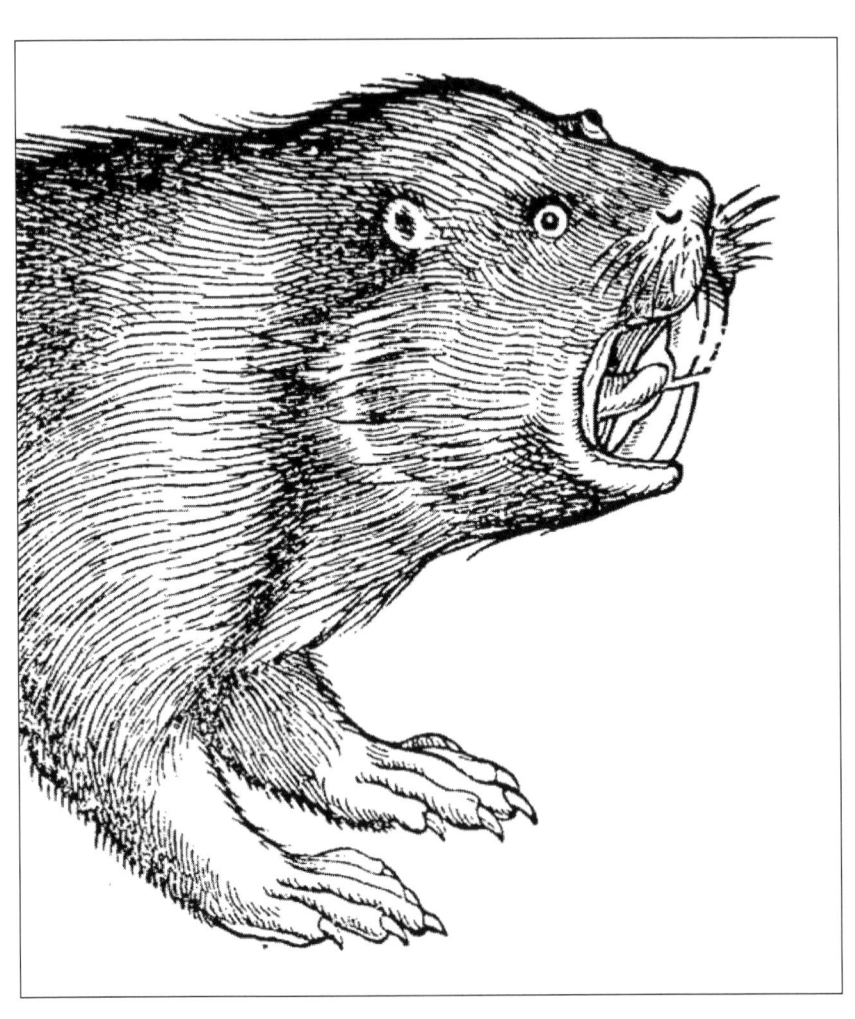

Foreword

Like many explorers, I always viewed Alaska as one of the last great frontiers. Sprawling mountain ranges tower over a vast pristine wilderness peppered with as many as three million lakes—and all completely skirted by a boundless, incomprehensible Pacific coastline, including countless unexplored islands. There are literally places where no man has set foot. The sheer immensity of the landscape is staggering.

So, when I had an opportunity to co-host the television series *Missing in Alaska* for the History Channel in 2015, I jumped at the opportunity. As you might expect, the mysterious Land of the Midnight Sun boasts a plethora of potential cryptids and monster legends, mostly well-chronicled by many diverse Native cultures. And like the rest of the Northwest Pacific Coast, Bigfoot traditions are plentiful with numerous names stemming from varied tongues—*Arulataq, Gagiit, Gilyuk, Nant'inaq, Toonijuk, Tornit, Urayuli*. Virtually all of these monikers translate literally to "Hairy Man" or "Bush Man" and describe a race of giant, hairy savages said to inhabit the forest. There is also the *Kushtaka*, which may also be a Sasquatch, though the Tlingit tribe largely views this creature as a type of shapeshifter—transforming lost travelers into a race of cursed otter men.

There are also accounts of malevolent, hair-covered little people, werewolves and demon dogs, menacing snow monkeys, monster-sized bears, thunderbirds, colossal beavers, woolly mammoths and a huge "demon wolf" known as the *Amarok*. Some of these creatures could in reality represent survivors from the last Ice Age—prehistoric species that crossed over the once-present land bridge from Siberia and survived long beyond their time. Considering how little Alaska's landscape has changed over the past ten thousand years since the Pleistocene epoch, it's certainly not beyond the realm of possibilities.

And we must not forget the staggering amount of aquatic habitat and limitless potential it holds. Alaska's immense Lake Illiamna may be home to the most probable of all cryptids—enormous, silver fish said to be 30 feet long. Fur-covered, reptilian "Sea Serpent" carcasses have been known to wash up on the coastline from time to time, as well as a new species of mysterious beaked whale known as the Karasu. Less likely, but still intriguing stories speak of a mermaid known as the *Qalupalik* and a type of half-walrus, half-man.

Thus, I was excited to hear my friend and colleague David Weatherly was assembling a sorely-needed comprehensive volume on all of these alluring enigmas. An explorer in his own right, Weatherly is the right man for the job—a veteran monster hunter who has spent his life investigating and documenting strange legends. And now, I encourage you, dear reader, to follow along on an awe-inspiring journey—in the spirit of the great explorers of the past.

Ken Gerhard
Cryptozoologist

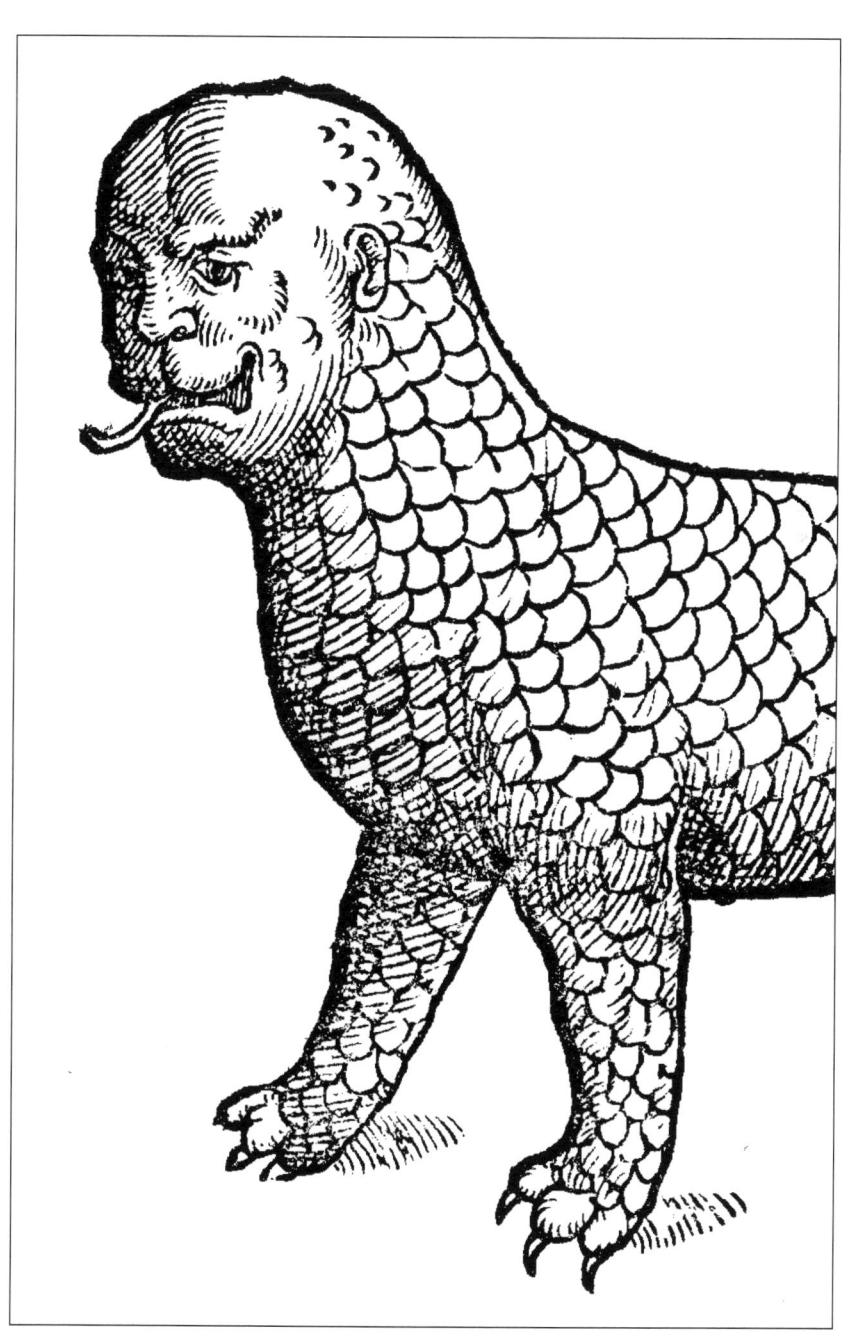

Introduction

Nicknamed "The Last Frontier," the state of Alaska is in the northwest extremity of the North American West coast, just across the Bering Strait from Asia.

By area, Alaska is the largest state in the union coming in at 663,268 square miles (256,089km²), much of it raw and rugged territory.

While it may rank first in size, the state ranks 48th in population. US statistics for 2018 revealed a total population of 737,438 people. Considering its size, Alaska rates as the most sparsely populated of the 50 states. As expected, the bulk of the population is clustered around cities, leaving vast tracks of unpopulated land.

Seventeen of the 20 highest points in the US are in the state, with the highest being Denali (formerly known as Mount McKinley), rising a staggering 20,310 feet (6,190 m) into the sky. For perspective, consider Pikes Peak down in the Lower 48 (as Alaskans refer to the rest of the nation.) Pikes Peak is at 14,115 feet (4,302 m), and if you're viewing it from Colorado Springs at 6,035 feet (1839 m)—you're looking at roughly 8,000 feet (2,438 m) of impressive rock. If you're looking at Denali from the Yentna River bank at 240 feet (73 m) above sea level, then you're basically seeing almost three Pikes Peaks stacked atop one another! It's a truly impressive vista, and almost otherworldly.

The lowest point in the state is at sea level. Alaska has a longer coastline than all other US states combined, and it shares a maritime border with Russia and land borders with the Canadian province of British Columbia and the Yukon Territory.

The state is resource abundant with an economy dominated by fishing, mining and the oil & gas industry. At its peak,

Alaska's North Slope produced more oil in one day than Texas did in a week, but production has tapered off with Alaska now being the nation's second-largest producer of petroleum.

The capitol is Juneau but approximately half of the state's residents live within the Anchorage metro area, the state's largest city.

Prior to US statehood, Alaska was a territory controlled by the Russians. In the 1860s, the United States and the Russian Empire entered treaty negotiations involving the territory. The process was overseen by then Secretary of State William Seward and Edourad de Stoecki, Russian Minister to the US. By the time things were settled in 1867, the United States had purchased Alaska for a total cost of 7.2 million dollars. The price equated to about two cents per acre and became known as "Seward's Folly," or "Seward's Icebox." The deal was considered foolish until the Klondike Gold Strike opened the door for the Alaskan gold rush. Between 1896 and 1899, an estimated 100,000 prospectors made their way to the Klondike region seeking their fortunes.

Fueled by the discovery of gold in the late 1800s, towns and cities grew as people rushed to the territory hoping to strike it rich. Rugged conditions didn't deter those with dreams of gold in their minds.

Alaska was organized as a US territory on May 11, 1912. It was finally admitted to the Union on January 3, 1959, becoming the 49th state.

Although there are no officially defined borders to demarcate the regions, it's widely accepted that there are five main regions in the state. They are commonly known as: Far North, Interior, Southcentral, Southwest and Southeast.

There's a common misconception that the entire state is permanently freezing cold and covered in snow, but there is some diversity. Climatic conditions in the far northern part of the state are artic, while the southeast is oceanic. The state's interior has recorded both the highest and lowest temperatures statewide (a high of 100° Fahrenheit, (38° Celsius), and low of -80° F (-62°C)).

Water resources are abundant in Alaska, with heavy snowfall and an abundance of lakes and rivers, so fresh water is easy to come by. There's an incredible array of wildlife that includes moose, Dall sheep, caribou, bears, mountain goats and salmon, just to name a few.

As for plant life, there's plenty of it, both wild and cultivated. It may surprise some to learn that the state's long summer days have led to the production of some unusually oversized produce. Examples harvested in recent years include a 35-pound broccoli (16 kilos), a 65-pound (29 kilos) cantaloupe and a cabbage coming in at 138 pounds (63 kilos)!

There's a certain quirkiness to Alaska and there are many truly unique things about the state. Dog mushing is the official state sport, and there's a museum dedicated to hammers. And please, if you're visiting the Last Frontier, don't give any beer to the moose—it's against the law.

Fascinating state facts aside, we're here to talk about monsters, and when it comes to Alaskan monster sightings, there are plenty.

Water monsters abound in the state. With an abundance of freshwater and the seas around it, there's plenty of room for strange creatures to dwell. From the well-known monster in Lake Iliamna, sightings of weird serpent-like things in the ocean, to First Nations legends of water creatures, Alaska has quite the variety of aquatic unknowns.

But it's not just Alaskan waters that hold mysteries. Giant birds have been sighted soaring over the state's skies. If the legendary thunderbirds are indeed living in North America, the northernmost state may be their hiding place.

Needless to say, Alaska has an abundance of sasquatch reports. The hairy giant has been spotted digging in the sand on beaches, swimming in the frigid waters, darting away into the thick forests and navigating deep snowbanks with no trouble.

Sasquatch has a rich history in Alaska. Native Alaskan tribes have long standing traditions involving the cryptid bigfoot. Called by a variety of names that often translate to terms such as "big man," or "hairy man," these beasts have been in the region as long as tribal memory.

It makes sense really. Despite modern developments, Alaska is still a "frontier" in many respects, and there's an abundance of unexplored territory. America's largest national forest is in the state. The Tongass National Forest was established in 1907 and covers an amazing 16.7 million acres (6.8 million hectares), more than three times the size of the next largest National Forest (which is also in Alaska). In short, there are tens of thousands of acres of wilderness, a perfect hiding place for large, undiscovered creatures to live.

There are other legends too. Legends of creatures from the past that some say still survive in the wilds of Alaska. Do mammoths still roam the tundra? Is there a dinosaur near Kodiak Island? And does a massive, prehistoric bear still prowl the snow-covered landscape? These and similar questions have lingered for years. Are the tales just fanciful stories or have ancient creatures really managed to hold on in small enclaves of the state's remote regions?

There's a certain mystery to Alaska, an otherworldly quality that's difficult to explain. The region has an intangible… something that affects some people on a deep level. Some of course, have no connection, no feeling other than the stark cold, while others journey to the rugged place only to fall in love with its uniqueness. Some simply enjoy the trip, while others remain entranced by something felt but undefined.

Perhaps bigfoot and the other creatures feel it too, or perhaps they just enjoy the solitude of the cold Alaskan climes.

I hope you enjoy this exploration into some of the rich cryptid history of Alaska. Grab your parka and join me on the trek as we delve into the monsters of the last frontier.

Alaska, Land of Mystery

PART ONE
Alaska's Weird Waters

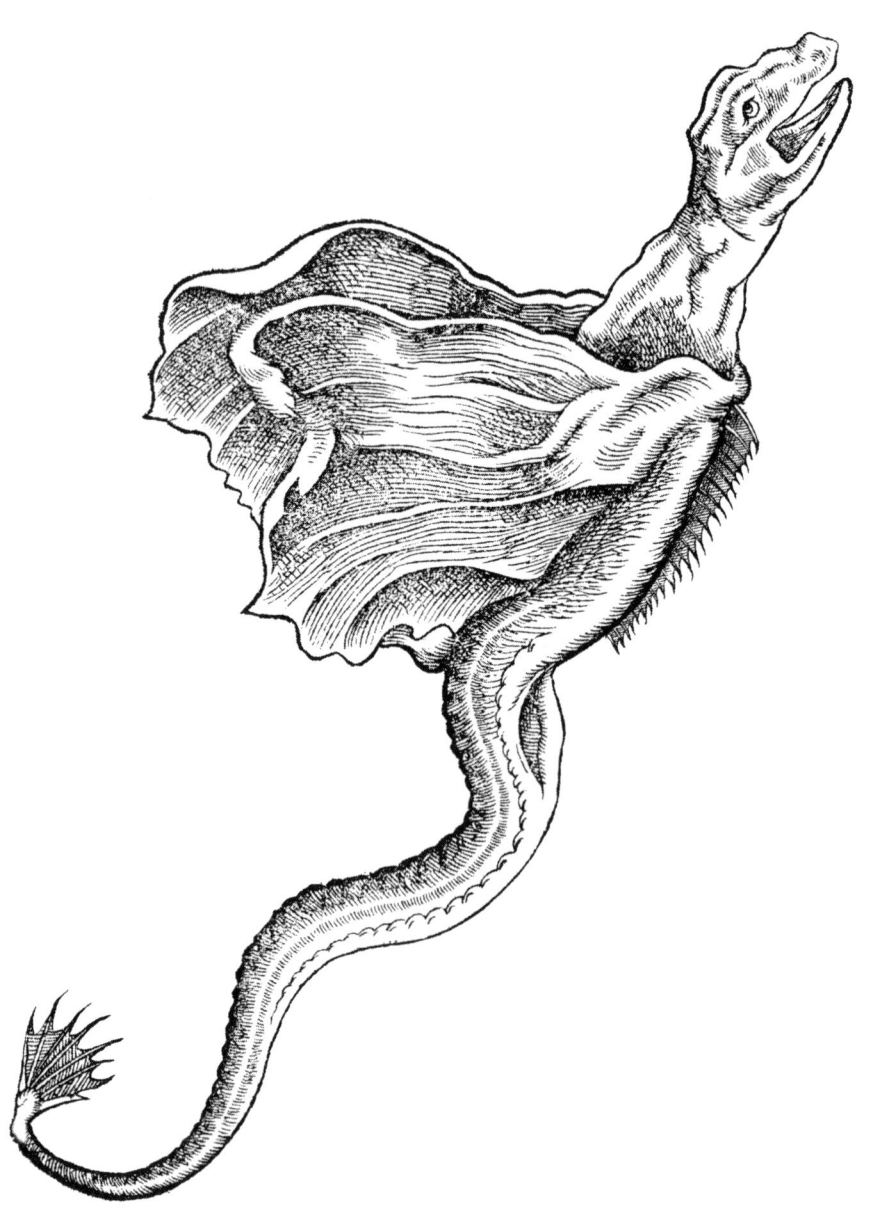

A Watery Land

Water, it seems, is everywhere in Alaska. The state is bordered by the Gulf of Alaska and the Pacific Ocean to the south and southwest, the Bering Sea, Bering Strait and the Chukchi Sea to the west and the Arctic Ocean to the north.

There are almost 34,000 miles (55,000 km) of tidal shoreline. One of the world's largest tides occurs in Alaska in Turnagain Arm south of Anchorage. Tidal differences of more than 35 feet (11 m) have been recorded.

The state gets ample rainfall and of course snowfall. Marshlands and wetland permafrost cover almost two hundred thousand square miles.

Glacier ice covers roughly 29,000 square miles, (47,000 km²) with the Bering Glacier—North America's largest glacier, covering just over 2000 square miles (3219 km²) alone.

And then there are the bodies of freshwater that dot the land. Alaska has a staggering three million lakes.

The state's most famous water monster, a giant living in Lake Iliamna, (discussed in detail later) has long been sought by monster hunters. Some believe they've determined the identity of the creature, but others feel it remains a mystery.

But with so many lakes, the tales of strange aquatic creatures is extensive. Cryptozoologist John Kirk lists a number of Alaskan lake monsters in his book *In The Domain of Lake Monsters*. Included are creatures in Lakes Crosswind, Kalooluk, Minchumina, Novinuk and Walker.

Cryptozoologist Loren Coleman mentions all of these along with Lakes Clark and Kaluluktok. Coleman also mentions monsters in several Alaskan rivers including the Buckland and Notak Rivers reportedly inhabited by the legendary Tirichuk.

Commercial fishing is a major industry in Alaska, and even before the waters were full of modern boats, native peoples of the region fished for sustenance. While the area is renowned for its salmon and king crab, a wide range of other fish are also caught, some of a pretty hefty size and weight.

Official state records list the largest halibut caught at 495 pounds (225 kilos), but the *Alaskan Dispatch* reported one that tipped the scales at 533 pounds (242 kilos), either way, it's a massive fish. Of course, there are always tales of "the one that got away" that was so much larger. In Alaska, that may indeed be reality and not just another fisherman's tall tale.

Large salmon are routinely caught with the official record being a Chinook Salmon caught in 1985 on the Kenai River. It weighed in at over 97 pounds (44 kilos).

The state's lakes have plenty of sizable fish too. The official record for trout is a 47-pound (21 kilos) catch from 1970, though natives have long stated there are much larger ones to be found. Chandler Lake in the north central portion of the state is said to be home to four-foot-long (1.2m) trout, as well as another mysterious aquatic creature described as 10 feet (3m) long, with great, black eyes. The fish, or whatever it is, is said to have dark coloring on top and red on its underside.

Fossil evidence found in Alaska verifies some of the creatures that lived in the region during the dinosaur age. In the summer of 2011, the fossil of a little-known sea going reptile was found near Kake in the Southeast portion of the state. The fossil was identified as a "thalattosaur" meaning "ocean lizard."

The existence of early creatures in the area may have had some bearing on native tales that passed down through the ages, and its clear that many of the state's aquatic mysteries have deep roots in the lore of the region's First Nations people. Tlingit tales speak of the *Gonakadet*, a strange creature that's part killer whale and part wolf.

The Inuit tell of the *Tizheruk*, and the *Pal-Rai-Yuk*, huge serpentine creatures that live in the ocean and attack ships. The creatures are also known to attack humans.

Writer Terrye Toombs says the creatures are a rich part of

Alaskan folklore:

"In mythology, the Tizheruk are large, snake-like sea creatures that are believed to roam Alaska's waters," Toombs wrote. *"They are described as having a head 7 feet* (2 m) *long with a tail ending in a flipper, for a total of 12 to 15 feet* (3.7 – 4.6 m) *long. Tizheruk were said to snatch people from docks and piers."*

Some accounts of the creatures claim they have legs or tentacles that they capture prey with. Inuit accounts state that the *Tizheruk* lived in the state's Buckland and Noatak Rivers. The creature was also said to lurk in the waters near King Island.

Another creature the Inuit said lived in the coastal waters of Nunivak Island was called the *Pal Rai Yuk*. Dr. John White of the Field Museum of Natural History talked to natives on Nunivak Island about the creature. They related various accounts and reported that the things were known to kill hunters and kayakers.

Reportedly, the creature had a head similar to a snake's and could raise its neck seven to eight feet (2 – 2.4 m) above the surface of the water.

The Inuit of western Alaska describe an aquatic predator known as the *"Az-i-wu-gum-ki-mukh-'ti,"* or Walrus Dog. The creature is said to be larger than an adult walrus and preys on fish and seals.

Those who have seen the creature say it's black in color. Some believe the creature is fur-covered while others state it's covered in scales. The animal is shaped like a dog but is elongated and slender. It serves as a protector of walrus colonies and uses its sharp-edged tail to slap the water when danger approaches.

Alaska also has its own mer-being legend. From the Inuit nation come tales of the *Qalupalik*, a creature that reportedly once lived in large numbers in the coastal waters of Alaska.

Tales of "mer-beings" are found around the world, the most famous being the classic mermaids of ancient lore who could use their siren's call to lure sailors to their deaths.

The Alaskan version of these creatures are described as

humanoids with greenish-gray skin, long human-like hair and long fingernails or claws. Their hands and feet are webbed to facilitate life in the ocean.

Tales of the *Qalupalik* are found mostly in coastal towns. They're supernatural creatures, a curious combination of mermaid and boogeyman. By some accounts, they are said to be rather shy, in other tales they are more aggressive and frightening.

The *Qalupalik* can swim rapidly underwater, rising to the surface on occasion. When they swim they make a great noise with the splashing of their arms and legs.

Much like the legendary mermaid of other cultures, the *Qalupalik* is said to have a strange song, one reportedly heard by hunters and people out on the ocean alone. The creatures could be seen in the summer basking in the sun on rocks, and in the winter sitting on the edge of ice floes. At times, they can be heard beneath the frozen surface, knocking on the ice. Kayakers are especially at risk if they run across the *Qalupalik* as the creatures will tip the vessel over and drag the victim into the depths.

It's said that hunters have killed the creatures on occasion, but the flesh is poisonous to humans, so they were never eaten.

It's also said that the *Qalupalik* wear an amauti made of eider duck skin. Traditionally, the amauti is a parka worn by Inuit women. It has a hood to shield against the cold winds and just below that, there's a built-in pouch to carry infants. The amauti worn by the *Qalupalik* has a more sinister purpose. The creatures are said to steal children and place them in the pouch, carrying them away to raise them as their own. In true, gruesome bogeyman tradition, other versions of the tales say the *Qalupalik* eat the children. In other stories, the creature takes the child away to a hidden cave, putting it to sleep and feeding on its energy over time.

Inuit elders tell children not to wander too close to the seashore, because the *Qalupalik* will come ashore and snatch them quickly. The creatures are also said to hum in a compelling fashion, a technique to lure young people close.

Accounts of the *Qalupalik* date back to at least the 1800s, but it's difficult to say how far back in Inuit lore the stories go. Some researchers believe tales of the creature were simply fabricated to keep children away from the dangerous waters, a utilitarian creation to help keep young ones safe from the dangers of the sea.

There is of course the chance that tales of the *Qalupalik* were inspired by some unusual, but very real, aquatic creatures.

Folklore and ancient tales aside, there are plenty of modern accounts of strange things in Alaska's waters. The area's most famous aquatic cryptid dwells in a glacial lake in the southwest portion of the state.

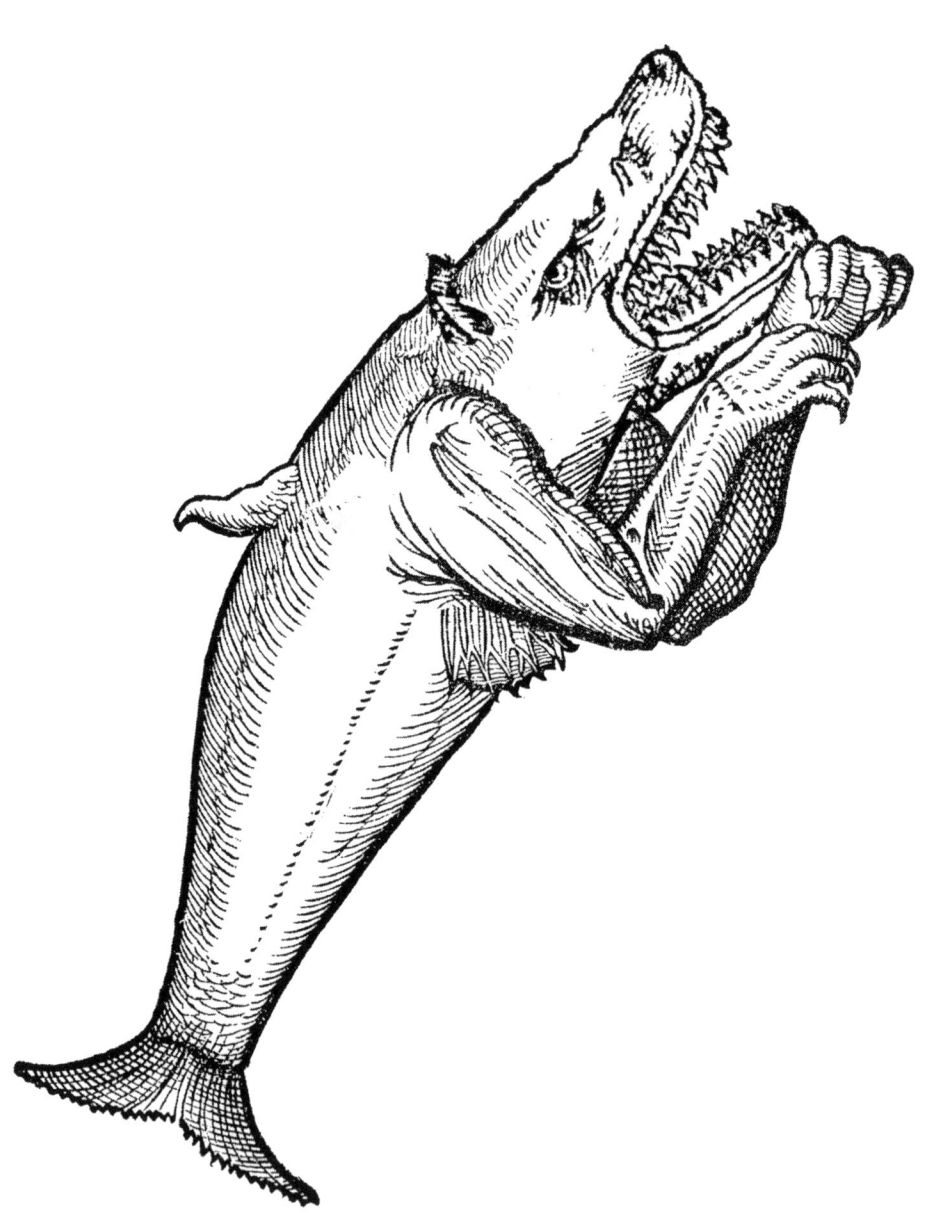

The Iliamna Lake Monster

Lake Iliamna is a large, natural lake in the southwest portion of the state. It's the largest lake in Alaska with a surface area of just over a thousand square miles (1610 km²).

The lake's average depth is 144 feet (44 m), but its deepest point reaches 988 feet (301 m). The Copper, Pile, Iliamna and Newhalen Rivers all flow into Lake Iliamna creating an estimated 9-12 thousand cubic feet (255 – 340 m²) of water flowing into the lake each second.

The lake is in a remote location, making it accessible almost exclusively by airplanes. Floatplanes are common throughout the state and during busy travel months they can been seen coming and going frequently on the lake's waters.

Small boats can also be used to reach the lake during the summer months and the area is a popular spot for hunters and fishermen, the primary economy for the area. The lake itself is well known for trophy fishing with several species of trout, arctic grayling, sockeye, Coho salmon and northern pike.

The lake is also home to the largest sockeye salmon run in the world, and the region around the lake has the largest brown bear population in the world, due in part, no doubt, to the abundance of salmon in the cold lake waters.

The area around Lake Iliamna is sparsely populated with less than a 1,000 residents living in the communities surrounding the glacial waters.

Although the area is remote, the lake and its surrounding rivers have been inhabited for centuries, and with its long history come tales of a monster in the water.

First Nations people in the region have long told tales of Lake Iliamna's strange beast, a massive creature that would attack men. Small boats and kayaks were said to be especially vulnerable to the thing that dwelled in the water's depths.

In the late 1700s, Russian fur traders heard the tales and reportedly had their own experiences with the creature. But history aside, there are plenty of modern accounts of the lake's monster, and people in the small fishing village of Iliamna are well familiar with the lore of the creature.

Locally, the monster has become known as "Illie," though opinions vary as to what the creature actually is. Some think it's just a giant fish, others believe it's something more unusual, a survivor from a prehistoric age, or a still-undiscovered aquatic species.

Illie is reported to be between ten and 30 feet (3 - 9 m) in length. Its head is square, and legend says its head is so solid and strong that the creature uses it to ram small boats, causing them to capsize.

First Nations lore offers several potential explanations for the creature's identity, all of them of course, rooted in tribal legend and tradition.

The Tanaina peoples said a giant black fish lived in the waters. According to them, the creature had powerful jaws and could bite holes in canoes.

Inuit legends say the giant fish in the lake are dangers to look at. Humans who look at them would shrivel up and die.

The Aleuts also mentioned the aquatic monsters of Lake Iliamna. They called the creatures the "*Jig-ik-nak*," and said the things hunted in packs. The Aleuts feared the creatures and said they were dangerous fish-like beings known to attack canoes and kill hunters.

From the Tlingit, there are tales of the *Gonakadet*. A beast with a body like an orca and a head and tail like that of a wolf. By some accounts, the *Gonakadet* was a human who had transformed into a lake monster and saved his village from starvation. The *Gonakadet* was recorded in ancient pictographs along the Alaskan and British Columbian coasts.

On the lake's eastern end, the Kenaitze tribe view the

monster as an ill omen. Children are warned to stay well away from the water's edge, lest the giant beast snap them up in its huge mouth.

One curious bit of lore involving the monster is that it hates the color red and will attack anything bearing the color. Early travelers were cautioned not to use red on their boats, lest they provoke the creature into attacking.

While these beasts may sound like pure fiction to modern ears, it's important to remember that the tales likely have roots in reality, and the people were interpreting the monster through their cultural lens. Early settlers to Alaska would have heard the stories and considered the tales in conjunction with what they themselves were seeing in the lake.

Lake Iliamna is frequently reached by Floatplane

Decades of Sightings

1940s

When air travel increased in Alaska and more small planes began flying to and from the lake, sightings of the creature increased. Some pilots even began flying lower over the water hoping to spot the animal.

In September 1942, bush pilot Babe Alsworth, accompanied by fisherman Bill Hammersley, were flying over the lake on their way to the village of Iliamna. The men spotted a pair of large specks in the water estimated to be about 40 feet (12 m) deep. Curious about what the specks were, they circled around for another look and determined that the objects were huge fish. The men said the fish were dull aluminum in color and had tapered bodies, wide heads, and vertical tails that swished from side to side. The men initially thought the fish were around ten feet in length.

Alsworth took the plane down for a closer look at the creatures. Dropping down from 1,000 to 300 feet (305 – 91 m), the pair quickly realized they had underestimated the size of the animals. The fish were longer than the plane's pontoon and had the appearance of mini submarines. The fish circled several times then surged in the water and vanished in the depths, leaving a wave of disturbance in their wake.

A few years later, in 1945, Larry Rost, a U.S. Coastal and Geographic Survey pilot, was flying 100 feet (30 m) above the lake when he saw a massive fish. Rost reported a dull aluminum-colored creature around 20 feet (6 m) in length.

1950s

The 1950s brought more reports of the monster and news of the creature caught the attention of the legendary Tom Slick. Slick had made his fortune from the Oklahoma oil boom in 1910, and by the 1950s was actively hunting cryptids around the world. Slick traveled to the lake to search for the monster, but he and his team didn't come away with any evidence.

Cryptozoologist and author Loren Coleman interviewed

Alsworth, who had worked with Slick during the search. Alsworth was already familiar with the creature due to his 1942 sighting. When Coleman spoke with the man in 1998, Alsworth confirmed the fish he saw were swimming in water that was only 40 feet (12 m) deep. He also related information about Slick's search, telling the cryptozoologist about the hunter's efforts. As Coleman writes:

"...Tom Slick had several times hired him to fly Slick and his boys to moose-hunting sites, and in the fall of 1959 to seek out the Monsters of Lake Iliamna. Slick had offered a reward of $1,000 to anyone who could catch one of the mystery creatures, and Slick himself was in charge of getting lines set with barrels for buoys. He even hired a helicopter to hover over the exact spot where Alsworth had his encounter. But Alsworth and Slick never saw the big unknown animals on these flights, and, indeed, said that he went over that place in the lake more than 100 times without seeing them again."

The January 1959 issue of *Sports Afield* included an article by Gil Paust on the lake monster. Titled "Alaska's Monster Mystery Fish," the article chronicled more than 30 years of sightings. Paust himself even went on an expedition to try to catch the monster. Loren Coleman writes about the attempt:

"...along with Iliamna Lake Monster hunters Slim Beck, John Walatka, and Bill Hammersley, used a Bushmaster seaplane as a dock and some homemade monster-fishing gear. The four attempted to catch the big one with a hook made from a foot-long, quarter inch-thick iron rod baited with a chunk of moose flank. Their line was several hundred feet of 16-inch stainless-steel aircraft cable. A 55-gallon oil drum was the bobber.

But the thing snapped the line."

Note that it requires 440 pounds (200 kilos) of force to submerge a 55-gallon (208 liters) drum.

1960s-1970s

Other sightings continued through the 1960s and 1970s. NASA astronauts on training flights over Alaska saw huge fish in the lake.

A geologist flying over the lake in 1960 reported seeing

four fish measuring ten feet (3 m) in length.

Another scientist, a state wildlife biologist, saw a giant fish in the lake in 1963. The creature was just below the surface and was estimated between 25 - 30 feet (8 – 9 m) in length.

Alaskan missionary Chuck Crapuchettes had two sightings of the lake's monster. In 1967, while flying a float plane over the lake, he spotted a huge animal in the water. He quickly got on the radio and tried to call for someone nearby who could verify the sighting, but no one was able to respond before the creature vanished.

One of Crapuchettes' friends tried to catch the monster. He used 5/16" (7.9 millimeters) stainless steel cable with #2 tuna hooks and baited them with caribou meat. The man tied the lines off on the struts of his floatplane and drifted around the lake. Suddenly, his plane was jerked, and he was knocked off the floats. The plane itself was towed off and the man barely made his way to shore. He had to walk for miles while the plane was being towed around the lake by whatever he'd hooked.

When he finally recovered his aircraft, the hooked cables were gone. The hooks on the remaining cables were straightened out. The heavy metal hooks were eight to nine inches (20 – 23 centimeters) in length, so straightening them out was no simple task.

Some people speculated that the man had hooked a whale. There have been reports that Beluga whales have gone up the Kvichak River and into the lake, so it is a possibility. However, the man did not report seeing a whale or any other creature surface for air during the incident.

In 1977, a pilot flying over Pedro Bay, at the northeast end of the lake, spotted a large fish on the surface. He estimated the length to be 12 - 14 feet (3.7 – 4.2 m). As the man observed, the animal dove beneath the surface, flashing a vertical tail as it did so.

Veteran air taxi pilot Tim LaPorte also spotted the giant fish in 1977 while flying over the lake. LaPorte had two passengers on board his plane when he spotted the fish lying still on the water's surface. LaPorte took the plane closer to get a better look at the creature. He said it was between 12 - 14 feet (3.7 – 4.2 m) in length and dark gray or brown in color. When the plane got closer, the fish dove beneath the surface and was quickly out of sight.

The sighting was actually LaPorte's second experience with the giant, sort of. In 1968, he was a passenger on another plane when two people on board saw the animal. LaPorte himself wasn't able to get a look at the beast due to where he was sitting.

There was still a lot of interest in the lake monster through the 1970s. In 1979, the *Anchorage Daily News* offered a reward to anyone would could provide conclusive evidence of the fish's existence. But the monster remained elusive and no one was able to collect the bounty.

1980s-1990s

George Wilson, a resident of the lakeside village of Igiugig, at the southwestern end of the lake, reported a sighting in 1985. Wilson was cleaning windows when he saw a huge fish swimming in the Kvichak River (the drainage of Lake Iliamna). Wilson described the creature as black in color with a dorsal fin at least three feet (0.9 meter) long.

Another lakeside resident, Verna Kolyaha, reported seeing a massive black fish in 1987. The fish had a white stripe down its fin. More locals reported a similar fish the following year.

A man on a fishing trip to the lake in 1992 saw the giant. His description was similar to previous accounts, a giant "something" silver-gray in color. The man said he pulled his line out of the water fearing the idea of ending up in a battle with what he thought was a 12-foot-long (3.7 m) creature.

Locals have told me that sightings continued on a regular basis through the late 90s and up to present day. Consistent reports drew another monster hunter to the site, and this one came with a camera crew.

River Monsters Arrives

In 2010, Jeremy Wade, star of the hit Animal Planet show, River Monsters, journeyed to Lake Iliamna in search of the creature. Wade collected a number of accounts from locals, some of which he related in his book *River Monsters*. One account came from native Bill Trefon:

"The next story I heard was from Bill Trefon, a native Alaskan of the Dena'ina tribe who lives on the shore of Lake Clark. One day in 1957 his parents were out on the lake when there was an impact and their motor stopped. Bill's father pulled up the motor to inspect it, and while he was doing this, his wife saw a large tail break the surface behind the boat. But this wasn't the most extraordinary thing. 'There were teeth marks on the propeller,' said Bill."

Trefon's mother estimated the fish was between ten and 12 feet (3 – 3.7 m) in length.

During his expedition to Lake Iliamna, Wade met with anthropologist Robbin LaVine who was studying subsistence fisheries on the lake, and had her own sighting of something large in the lake. She and a colleague were in a float plane when they spotted the animal. As Wade recounts:

"Robbin says she observed the animal for a good thirty to forty seconds. Far too big to be a seal, she said it was 'distinctly fishlike' with a long, broad head and large pectoral fins, giving a profile somewhat like an arrowhead. She said it wasn't on the surface: 'It almost looked like it might have been stirring up something on the bottom, although there were no clouds of silt.'"

LaVine told Wade she estimated the length of the fish to be the same as one of the aluminum skiffs used on the lake—at least 15 feet (4.6 m).

Theories

After his investigation and time at the lake, Jeremy Wade came to the conclusion that the mysterious monster is a sturgeon.

"There's one more thing that makes me think the Iliamna monster is a sturgeon. While filming near the village of Nondalton on the river between Lake Clark and Lake Iliamna, we met with three lads fishing

in a boat who had seen the first series of River Monsters and were curious to know what we were doing here. I said we were investigating the monster and asked if they had any ideas about what it was.

'Yeah, it's a sturgeon,' one of them said."

White sturgeon are powerful fish and have been known to leap out of the water and accidentally hit boats. They can grow to a massive 20 feet (6.1 m) in length and weigh up to 1,799 pounds (816 kilos). Sturgeon have a long lifespan and spend most of their time on the water's bottom, making sightings of the fish fairly rare.

Over the years, numerous people have reported the propellers of their boats damaged by what appear to be teeth marks. The damage may be more support for the sturgeon theory, since the fish have teeth-like armor plating on their backs.

Tales of boats being overturned by creatures in the water could also be attributed to the sturgeon.

Other theories suggest the monster is a Pacific sleeper shark. In Alaska, the species can reach lengths of 20 feet (6.1 m) and weigh up to four tons (3.6 tonnes). Sleeper sharks have thrived in recent years, becoming a dominant predator in both the North Pacific and Arctic oceans. They're known scavengers and also feed on a range of fish and marine animals. Scientists note that nearly every marine species in the Arctic ocean has been found in the stomachs of sleeper sharks.

Sleeper sharks are quiet predators, able to glide through the water with little body movement and little hydrodynamic noise.

Sleeper sharks have been spotted in freshwater and in shallow water. Marine biologists believe the sharks are capable of using freshwater lakes for food and refuge. Discoveries are still being made about the species and their behavior, making them a possible candidate for Lake Iliamna's mysterious denizen.

Mythical monster? Giant, but known fish species? Ultimately, the jury is still out on the monster's true identity.

While both the sturgeon and the sleeper shark are good candidates, neither have been verified to live in Lake Iliamna.

Sightings continue and people still search for Illie, and perhaps someday in the near future, the true nature of the creature will finally be revealed. But a native man I spoke with doesn't believe it will be so easy:

"Whatever it is, it's been there a long, long time, maybe before people were here. Maybe we won't ever find it unless it lets us find it. When the right person with the right spirt seeks it, then it will be found."

The Kodiak Dinosaur

April 15, 1969. A 65-foot (20 m) fishing vessel named the *M.V. Mylark* was operating off the coast of Raspberry Island in the Shelikoff Strait near Kodiak Island. The vessel was outfitted with a Simrad EH2A, the day's top-of-the-line sonar device.

The sonar was used by commercial fishing boats to locate and track schools of fish. As standard procedure, the sonar was left running while the ship was in operation.

One of the operators noticed a very unusual readout from the device and managed to capture a printout of the image, an image that appeared to show an animate, and very large, dinosaur-like creature.

Whatever the thing was, it was sitting about 300 feet (91 m) below the water's surface. The creature appeared to have a finned, long-necked body. The *Mylark's* captain, Chet Peterson, later estimated the object was about 200 feet (61 m) in length.

The incident made local news, hitting the front page of the *Kodiak Daily Mirror* on April 30th with a questioning headline: "A Sea Monster?"

Captain Stanley Lee sent a clipping about the monster to his friend Ivan Sanderson who became intrigued by the case. Sanderson obtained a copy of the original printout from the Simrad system captured by the *Mylark*. The echogram showed a large silhouette with dinosaur-like features, just like the ship's crew reported.

The experienced crew were astonished by what the sonar detected. As Ivan Sanderson noted:

"Imagine the sonar operator's surprise when the machine suddenly presented him with a clear silhouette of an enormous 'creature' between 150 and 180 feet (46 – 55 m) long, with two pairs

of flippers, an extended tapering tail, and a long, slender neck capped by a rather snub-nosed head!"

Unfortunately, there are currently no known copies of the sonar print-out that captured the unusual image. Researchers have noted that the description of the creature matches the long extinct plesiosaur.

Sanderson took the image to the manufacturers of the Simrad device to get their opinion on the anomaly. Representatives of the company, Supervisors Incorporated (the U.S. subsidiary of the Norwegian-based Simrad company), were hesitant to say much about the readout but apparently tried to dissuade Sanderson from putting too much stock in the reading. Sanderson's point of contact told him:

"You certainly got hold of a very exciting echogram there, but I'm afraid that I will have to disappoint you as to the credibility of what you see on it. It has a couple of defects which make its genuineness questionable."

At the least, it was an odd statement from someone representing the technology. The man went on to tell Sanderson that other factors may have changed the readout including the boat's speed. The representative went further and suggested a crew member may have modified the image on the readout which could change the interpretation.

In other words, there was a subtle suggestion that someone was perpetrating a hoax.

Sanderson wasn't impressed with the comments from the Simrad company rep and noted that the implication of a hoax on the part of the equipment operator was absurd. The investigator pointed out that the strip of graph paper was still in the machine when the Captain retrieved it just after the hit. Obviously, the printout hadn't been tampered with by the man monitoring the equipment.

Going the extra mile, Sanderson consulted a total of 14 other experts from various fields including Naval Operations, law enforcement and oceanography, and had them review the printout. They all agreed it had not been tampered with.

Sanderson felt that officials at Simrad wanted to discredit any possibility of a water monster and chose to focus on the possibility of a hoax in order to do so. But why go to such trouble? The investigator had some thoughts to explain the company's mindset:

"Why do the manufacturers of Simrad seem bent upon discrediting our Alaskan long neck echogram? Perhaps they are simply trying to protect the good name of their product; after all, since science says that sea monsters do not exist, scientists might accuse the instrument that detects one of being faulty."

Roy P. Mackal weighed in on the sonar reading as well, noting there was a possibility of a flaw in the radar, but he was equally open to the idea that an unknown creature could have been captured:

"There were often skeptics who claimed sonar readings in Loch Ness were the result of the sound waves bouncing back from the loch sides. Not all readings can be attributed to this, but some possibly could. Could the same thing have occurred here but with the waves bouncing back from the ocean floor? I am no sonar expert, so I don't know if it is possible. The other explanation is that it was a huge, strange, unknown creature, which is always a possibility."

Sanderson considered the Alaskan sonar capture a significant piece of evidence and remained adamant that the Simrad reading was an authentic capture of an unknown animal. As he wrote:

"Well, I for one am convinced that, (1) Simrad is not faulty, (2) the echogram is perfectly authentic and (3) somewhere in the icy waters of the southern coast of Alaska there's at least one monstrous marine long neck swimming around—and who knows how many more?"

Another possible sighting of the same creature occurred a few years later in Uyak Bay. In the summer of 1971, a fishing crew sighted a large sea creature that none of them recognized. Witnesses estimated the creature was around 30 feet (9 m) long and said that it had a head like a horse. Crew member Eddie Pakkanin later stated:

"We don't know what it was, but it had a grayish color and we

couldn't see any fins, or any tail and it never made any noise. It would just come up and you could see the head and part of the body."

Kodiak High School's oral history magazine, *Elwani*, wrote about the sighting in a 1977 issue of the publication. The article included comments from another witness who had been on board the vessel that day. According to the second man, the creature was closer to 40 feet (12.2 m) in length:

"...with dull brown color, and it did have hair, sort of like sea lions, but not as thick. It had a real narrow and long head, kind of horse shaped with two nostrils. When it came up, the head and the neck and part of the back came up, with water covering the middle part and then the tail would come up."

Eddie Pakkanin reported that another man on board, DeWitt Fields, fired at the creature with a rifle at which point the animal dove beneath the surface and swam under the craft. The crew watched in fascination as the creature resurfaced on the opposite side of their vessel then swam away.

Fields' wife, Wanda, captured a photo of the creature that was published in *Elwani*. The grainy picture depicts something large but partially submerged moving across the surface of the water. A witness who was on board the day of the sighting told the *Elwani* that the photo depicted a long snout that was skimming the water ahead of the creature's eye and the nape of the neck, sloping down into the back.

Eddie Pakkanin said the creature showed up for several more days, each time at about two in the afternoon before it vanished for good.

Another person on the skiff told the *Elwani* interviewer that he'd seen the creature again two or three years after the '71 sighting. He and his family had closed up camp for the season and were loading their skiffs for the 100-mile (161 kilometers) trek back to town. Witnesses spotted the strange animal while they were on the beach:

"If we hadn't been trying to beat the tide we would have gone out for a better look, but we were pressed for time."

As of the interview, the man had not seen the creature on

any other occasions. Whatever the thing was, it seemed to only linger in an area for so long before it disappeared back into the depths or moved further out to sea.

In 2002, the crew of a fishing boat spotted a similar creature off the west coast of Kodiak Island. It was around 4 a.m. when the men saw the animal in the water. The men were in a 22-foot (7 meter) skiff headed out for their gillnet a quarter of a mile out.

Dave Little was piloting the boat with Tollef Monsen and another unnamed crewman on board. It had been a busy fishing season and the men had made the same run numerous times already that year.

But this day would prove different.

Moving over the water, heading for the net, the men spotted something unusual. About two boat lengths away, an animal put its head up out of the water. As Monsen later stated:

"There's this neck and head, and it wasn't like your hands around the neck big, it was like your arms around the neck big."

Little noticed the creature as well, though he was busy trying to pilot the boat and could not focus on the thing directly. He stated:

"I saw it do its movements, but I couldn't tell you if the neck was a foot (0.3m) in diameter or three feet (1m) in diameter. It was all darkish, but I was paying attention to driving the skiff."

Despite the early morning hour, there was still enough light for the men to see the creature clearly enough to tell it wasn't something they'd ever seen before. The animal, whatever it was, wasn't interested in the fishing skiff though. As Monsen noted:

"It didn't really focus on us. It didn't look at us, it didn't make eye contact, no. And whatever it was didn't stick around. In a few seconds—it was seconds—it was gone, back under the water. I mean we were so tired that it was like, did I just see that? Did we just see that?"

Monsen believes he encountered the water monster again the following summer. He was by himself on the occasion, cleaning out the holding skiff while Little and the other crewman were out to pull in a net. It was a calm and sunny day and Monsen was focused on his work when something rammed the bottom of the skiff.

"All of a sudden it was like DONG! And the skiff kind of lurches, and I'm like what the hell was that? It was big, like a log. But nothing goes DONG! And lurches this big old skiff like that. I don't know what that was either."

The hit was so hard it almost knocked Monsen overboard, though he didn't spot the creature when it happened. He said there were no whales in the area, or anything known to be large enough to cause such a hit on the vessel. The craft was anchored at the time of the incident.

Are all these sightings of the same creature, or members of the same family of aquatic animals? Maybe the cold waters around Kodiak are holding a monstrous secret.

First Nations fishing group 1935

Sea Serpents & Other Aquatic Oddities

The frigid seas and oceans around Alaska are home to a diverse range of marine life but some of it may be undocumented to this day. Tales of sea serpents and weird aquatic creatures go far back in the region's history.

One early report dates back to the fall of 1900 when a man named Knugg Johansen of Wrangell spotted a strange creature in the Bering Sea. Johansen said he told the story once, but the person he related it to laughed about the incident. As a result, Johansen refused to discuss the incident for years. He finally agreed to talk about the sighting in 1944 when he did an interview with the *Wrangell Sentinel*. Here's the account he gave to the paper:

"In the year of 1900, I was working for an Alaskan fish canning company on the Nushagak River in Alaska. We had finished our pack on August first, and I was put aboard a small steamer as deckhand for our trip to our home port, which was Astoria, Oregon.

At midnight on the tide we left the harbor and after steaming six or seven hours, we were about eighty nautical miles in the Bering Sea. At 8 a.m. it was my turn at the wheel and after having had my breakfast, I went to relieve the other man. He and the captain left for the galley to have their breakfast, which left me alone in the wheelhouse.

The weather was absolutely the finest you could imagine, bright sunshine, no wind—not a ripple in the water.

At this time while looking out across the water, I perceived about 150 feet (46m) off the port bow a large animal or fish partially submerged, floating on the water. It was an unusual sight and at that time impressed me so greatly that its every feature is indelibly imprinted on my mind.

I will now describe it as I saw it on that perfectly clear day. I judged the animal or fish to be about twenty-five feet long (7.6m) and about fifteen inches (38cm) in diameter at the largest part. The main body was the color of kelp, and the tail was a little lighter shade than the rest of the body. The mane was darker than either. The head was out of the water and the tail, or the end of the body, was entirely out of the water when I first saw it. The forehead protruded greatly from the lower part of the face. The eyes were jet black and big and round. From the eyes down the face was more the shape of the faces of cattle, but from the eyes up and back, the face was the exact shape of a horse's face. I could not see how far down the body the mane reached.

The end of the fish or animal was above the water about five feet (1.5m). This end was a little smaller in diameter than the rest of the body, but not much smaller. There was nothing such as fins, legs, or feet, appended to this part of the body.

In a little while, through movement, other parts of the body became visible. I hollered for someone to come up and observe the object, but it was visible above the water for about half a minute. The tail sank below the water first and the middle of the body came out so that I could see between the ocean and the middle part of the body. This part was about ten feet (3m) long. There were no fins, feet, or any apparent means of locomotion.

As we got closer diagonally to the fish or animal, it started to sink. The middle of the body went down. Then the head rose so I could see more of it than I had at first. I could not see any nostrils. The whole animal than sank smoothly. There was not a ripple on the water. The last to disappear was the end of the tail, then the snout — then all was calm.

About that time the skipper came up and wanted to know what I was hollering about. I knew that it was of no avail as there was no way to prove what I had seen, so I said, 'Oh, nothing, just something I saw.'

The sight was so strange and clear that it seems best that I record it. I am getting along in years now and feel that I should let some institution know of my experience so that from my description of its shape and color, a drawing could be made of the fish or animal so that people could understand it and visualize what I saw."

Another veteran sailor spotted a weird creature in Alaskan waters years later. Frank Reed spotted the anomaly in waters off southeastern Alaska. His story was published in the September 1944 edition of *Alaska Life* magazine.

"Frank Reed had spent many years at sea on sailing vessels and had seen many strange sea animals, but he had never seen anything before or since that compared with the creature he saw in Southeastern Alaska several summers ago.

At that time, Mr. Reed was watchman on a fish trap and lived in a shack on the beach. On this particular day, he was working on his boat, anchored somewhat down from the trap. He heard an unusual amount of splashing, but thought it was the fish trying to escape the trap. The noise was so persistent that Reed turned toward the trap and was astounded to see the most amazing sea creature that he had ever seen. It was tearing at the trap netting with long curved claws. He watched the creature for several minutes, long enough to get a detailed image in his mind.

The thing had a round head approximately the size of a human head which it held stiffly erect as it tore at the netting. The neck was about the same proportions to the head. The "shoulders" were narrower than the shoulder of a man, and the body tapered down to a serpent-like tail. The arms were about the size of a large man and ended in claws approximately four or five inches (10 -13cm) long.

Suddenly the creature sighted Reed. It loosed its hold on the net and dropped instantly into the water. Then the most astounding thing happened. The sea creature surfaced a few feet from the trap and swam away at a very rapid rate. It did not swim nor dart like a fish, but made long, powerful, overhead strokes with those powerful arms much like a swimmer."

Pennock Island Sea Serpent

Pennock Island is at the southern end of the Alexander Archipelago near Ketchikan. In 1947, a strange creature was reported by a pair of witnesses who were rowing around the island's north point.

Lauri Carlson and a friend were out on the water on May 8th when the animal surfaced about 25 feet (7.6m) from their boat. Carlson reported that the creature's head resembled a cow's but smaller. The creature's neck was estimated at eight inches

(20.3cm). It submerged in seconds and a line of fins became visible. The fins resembled a serrated crest and was along the creature's back. No estimate of the animal's length was given by witnesses.

Nushagak Bay Monster

In June 2007 a fisherman captured video of an odd something swimming in Nushagak Bay. Kelly Nash caught footage that appeared to show a large, serpent-like creature or creatures in the ocean waters.

Nushagak Bay, it should be noted, is adjacent to Kvichak Bay where the river drains from Lake Illiamna. Some researchers speculate that "Illie" travels these waterways on a regular basis.

Nash was out with his sons, Kyle and Jensen when they spotted a group of unknown animals being pursued by a pod of beluga whales. Paul Leblond and John Kirk reviewed the footage captured by Nash. According to the two researchers, the footage showed at least one animal that appeared to be a living version of the famous Naden Harbor carcass. *

*The Naden Harbor carcass was discovered at a whaling station at Haida Gwaii (commonly known as the Queen Charlotte Islands), in the summer of 1937. The remains were found in the stomach of a sperm whale and laid out on a five-foot table to be photographed. The carcass was about twelve feet (3.7m) in length with signs of a dorsal crest or vertebral column, short fore-flippers and a spade-shaped fluke. Witnesses who examined the carcass said the carcass had a discernible head that resembled a large dog with the features of a horse and the turned down nose of a camel. The creature's body was smooth though one witness claimed it was covered with a fur-like material. Sadly, the carcass was disposed of before it could be studied further. Three photographs of the carcass remain and have long puzzled researchers.

Paul LeBlond, former head of the Department of Earth and Ocean Sciences at the University of British Columbia, while known as an academic for his work in the field of ocean sciences, is also well known in the field of cryptozoology and was a former director of the International Society of Cryptozoology. LeBlond spoke with Discovery News about the footage:

"I am quite impressed with the video, although it was hot under rainy circumstances in a bouncy ship, it's very genuine."

LeBlond believes the video is evidence of a Cadborosaurus, a topic he's done extensive work on. (LeBlond and Edward Bousfield coauthored *"Cadborosaurus: Survivor From the Deep,"* a study of the ancient creature).

In 2012, the footage was set to air on the Discovery Channel's reality program "Alaskan Monster Hunt: Hillstranded" Oddly, the most significant footage never aired.

According to Leblond and cryptozoologist John Kirk, one sequence of Nash's footage was clear and impressive. According to an article on Cryptomundo:

"When the Nash footage was shown on Alaskan Monster Hunt, glaringly omitted from this program was the sequence containing the Naden Harbor lookalike turning its head to look full on at the camera."

Nash stated that he had no idea why the footage wasn't used in the program, but John Kirk wasn't fully satisfied with the response.

In December 2013, Kirk was approached to discuss the question of Canada's Ogopogo and the Cadborosaurus on MSNBC's news program "Caught on Camera." When asked for examples of footage to use for the show, Kirk suggested the Nash clip. Producers informed him they had already reached out to Nash only to learn that the footage had been sold to a production company. Kirk also learned that Kelly Nash had passed away in October 2013 leaving the destiny of the footage up to surviving family members.

Kirk stated that when he and Leblond viewed the footage, they had not seen it on the original Hi8 tape it was captured on. Kirk and Leblond viewed the footage at separate times on the same day, but both viewed it on a laptop computer and DVD player attached to a television.

Pursuing the mystery, Kirk reviewed the original correspondence from Kelly Nash dated May 2009. Nash had included a diagram of the area where the footage was captured along with a sketch of the creatures.

The diagram also showed something else interesting—the location of the camera. When Kirk examined the diagram closely, he found there were actually two cameras at the location. One was being manned by Kelly Nash, and the second by his son Kyle. A scenario dawned on Kirk that would explain the lack of the creature footage in the Discovery show. As further noted on Crypomundo:

"...what Kelly had possibly done was to sell the production company the footage from one camera while the footage from the other one was overlooked. It is most likely that the Naden Harbor creature sequence was not on the tape that went to the Hillstranded producers."

Apparently, the second camera was broken, making it so that video could be played in the camera but not removed. Further research revealed a bit of news from Kyle Nash. He reported that the camera had been given to a friend of his who may have taped over the footage of the water monster.

If this is indeed the case, it's a sad loss of what Kirk and Leblond state was amazing footage of an unknown creature in Alaskan waters.

One thread of hope is that Kelly Nash had DVDs made of the footage after he captured it. His son stated that he believes a box of the DVDs may still be around, but in the aftermath of his father's passing, he wasn't pressed to locate them.

Both John Kirk and NBC producers continued to follow up on the footage to no avail. John later told me that Kelly's son Kyle has no idea what happened to the lost footage. Perhaps at some point, one of the DVDs will turn up, but until then, the case remains another mystery in the annals of cryptozoology.

Aquatic Oddities

When doing research on monsters, other bits and pieces of legends often surface. Stories either long forgotten or distorted and changed far from their original tale emerge.

Supposedly, on Baranof Island, a giant beaver once ran amok and destroyed an entire village.

On a lake at the head of the Kobuk River, an Inuit man

The author exploring Alaska

watched a giant fish eat a caribou, a man and a canoe.

In late April 1947, Juneau Lumber Company tugboat operator Lou Baggnon saw a large creature in the water. Baggnon was piloting the *Suntrana* in Security Bay near Kuiu Island when the incident occurred. His wife was with him and also witnessed the creature. The couple said the animal "had a flat, goggle-eyed head and was looping along through the water" with vertical undulations.

On September 13, 1970, a witness named Manne Landstrom saw a creature 30 feet (9m) long that resembled a log. The beast had a flat head that resembled a crocodile. The *Kodiak Daily Mirror* reported the incident in its October 10th edition. Few details were available, but the sighting occurred at Big Lake north of Anchorage in Denali National Park.

Inuit tales also speak of a giant octopus that inhabited the Bering Strait. They called the creature the "*Amikuk*," and warned early explorers of its presence. There could be some truth to the stories since some scientists believe the Colossal Squid may live in the cold northern waters.

The remote area certainly holds a lot of secrets, and there's little doubt there are undocumented species in the region. Japanese legends have long spoken of a dark colored, beaked whale in the region.

In June 2014, an unusual carcass was found in the Pribilof Islands' community of St. George. A young biology teacher discovered the carcass on the beach and alerted a researcher in the area. The carcass was 24 feet (7.3m) long with dark flesh and a large, floppy dorsal fin. The animal's teeth were worn and yellowed with age. At first, it was assumed the body was that of a Baird's beaked whale, but closer examination proved that wasn't case.

Research published in 2016 verified the animal was an entirely new species, an odd-shaped black cetacean that Japanese fishermen called "*karasu*" or raven.

Phillip Morin, a scientist at the National Oceanic and Atmospheric Administration's Southwest Fisheries Science Center was excited about the find:

"It's just so exciting to think that in 2016 we're still discovering things in our world—even mammals that are more than 20 feet (6.1m) long. We don't know how many there are, where they're typically found, anything, but we're going to start looking."

Paul Wade of NOAA's National Marine Mammal Laboratory echoed Morin's excitement:

"'It's a really big deal. If you think about it, on land, discovery of new species of large mammals is exceptionally rare. It just doesn't happen very often. It's quite remarkable.'

Robert Pitman of the Society of Marine Mammalogy called the discovery of the whale 'heartening.'

'It boggles my mind to think that a large, very different-looking whale has gone unnoticed by the scientific community for so long. It sends a clear message about how little we know about what is in the ocean around us.'"

Perhaps the weirdest water cryptid report from Alaska was collected by cryptozoologist Bobbie Short. Short reported that a witness saw—of all things—a platypus in the coastal waters around Mountain Point near Ketchikan.

Short said the man was very familiar with aquatic life and "an experienced commercial fisherman." The man said the creature was about six feet (1.8m) in length, dark in color with an obvious bill and webbed feet.

J. Robert Alley, author of *Raincoast Sasquatch*, interviewed the witness in this case. He reports:

"Several years ago, Mike F., a successful Ketchikan businessman, contractor and retired fisherman asked me…whether I had ever studied or read anything about platypuses in North America, specifically whether I knew of any prehistoric giant forms. [Later he told me] that as a young man forty or so years ago he had stood on shore near Mountain Point south of Ketchikan and spent a minute watching an animal in the water at very close range that simply resembled a giant platypus. He described the creature as dark with a bill and feet like a platypus only the overall size was six feet or possibly greater. He gave no mention of the tail if there was one. The sighting was in shallow water on a rocky shoreline and the creature was close to the

surface. The man is an experienced commercial fisherman and stated categorically that it was not a known species of seal. Ocean temp here doesn't vary much from 50 degrees (10°C)."

The platypus is native to Australia, a far cry from Alaskan waters. Adult males of the species typically reach a length of 18 - 24 inches (46 – 61cm), making the one spotted in Alaska three times the size of the largest Australian example.

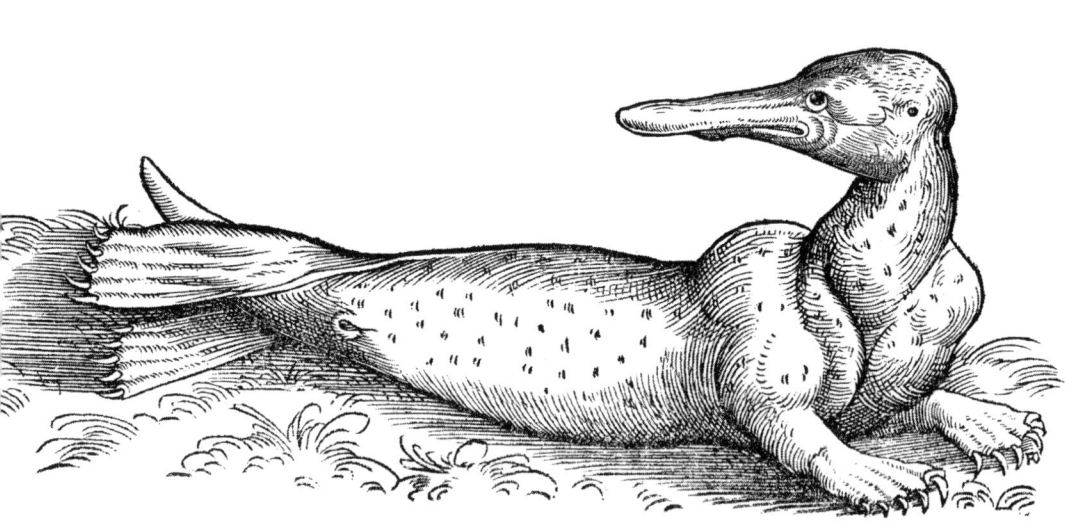

Globsters

"Globster" is a term for an unidentified organic mass that washes up from the ocean or a body of water. Globsters are notable for being unidentifiable, at least, during initial examination by untrained observers. The term was created by cryptozoologist Ivan T. Sanderson in 1962 and first applied to a carcass that washed up in Tasmania in 1960.

Due to the difficulty in identifying globsters, they are often dubbed "sea monsters." Frequently, scientists are able to identify the remains, though often the results are disputed, leaving some globsters as highly controversial.

Alaska has had its share of these weird masses over the years. In the fall of 1930, a mysterious carcass was discovered on the state's desolate Glacier Island in Prince William Sound. The *New York Times* reported on the incident in its November 26th edition under the headline: "Ice Bares Strange Animal; Alaskans Suggest Prehistoric Origin—Museum Here Investigating."

According to the *Times* report, the thing had a 20-foot (6.1m) body, a 16-foot (4.9m) tail and a six-foot (1.8m) head, all for a grand total of 42 feet (12.8m) in length. Two days later, rival paper the *New York Sun* added a statement that the creature had a "long snout."

As reports on the carcass came in, it also seemed to grow in size.

W.J. McDonald, supervisor of the Chugash National Forest, took a party to investigate the carcass. He found it in a degraded state, with little flesh remaining on it. Still, he estimated the creature's weight at 1,000 pounds (454 kilos) when it was living.

McDonald and his team did precise measurements on the carcass and reported that it had a head 59 inches (150cm) long and "much like that of an elephant." Other details of the report included:

"A snout that measured 39 inches(99cm) *from its tip to the center of the beast's forehead: it was 11 inches* (28cm) *long, with a 29-inch* (74cm) *circumference. The body measured 24 feet* (7.3m) *long, with a 14-foot* (4.3m) *tail. The rear-skeletal remains were 38 inches* (97cm) *wide at the broadest point."*

McDonald fueled the idea that the remains belonged to something prehistoric when he stated the creature was notable because of its *"long tail and tapering head, like a dinosaur."*

In January 1931, the *Ogden Standard-Examiner* out of Ogden, Utah ran a story that included a fanciful account of the creature's final moments. The reporter explored the idea that the beast was one from a long-ago age, and wrote that the animal *"...must have been encased before the general migration began."*

But was the carcass really that of a dinosaur left behind when its fellows ran off to warmer climes?

Several cryptozoologists over the years looked at the case but offered no opinion due to the scant information available, and the identity remained elusive for many years.

Dr. Karl Shuker finally solved the riddle in September 2010. Shuker traced the path of the carcass and discovered it had been purchased in January 1931 for 600 dollars. The buyer was the owner of a taxi company who put the monstrous remains in a traveling carnival. The mysterious carcass traveled around North America for a time until if finally landed at the Smithsonian Institution's National Museum of Natural History in Washington, D.C. It was eventually identified by scientists as the remains of a minke whale. A disappointing ending for those who fancied the creature was something more mysterious, but at least the puzzle was solved. The same can't be said for a mass of organic something found several years later.

In 1946, the remains of another presumed prehistoric monster were found on the Kenai Peninsula. According to a report in the October 25th edition of Michigan's *Traverse City Record-Eagle*, the body was that of a *"huge, lizard-like creature identified tentatively as a prehistoric tyrannosaurus or gorgonosaurus."*

The paper reported that anthropologists from the University of Alaska at Fairbanks were headed to the site to investigate the find. Doctors in Fairbanks had examined the carcass and declared that it was *"definitely prehistoric,"* so there was some excitement in the air.

It was believed the remains had been preserved in glacial ice until they washed ashore. According to the *Record-Eagle*, the creature:

"...measured nearly nineteen feet(5.8m) *from tip to tail. Its head measured 2 feet by 2 ½ feet* (0.6 to 0.8m) *and its mouth featured a row of teeth 18 inches* (46cm) *long.*

The animal had large hind legs and a heavy thigh bone which measured approximately 4 feet (1.2m) *from the hip to the first joint. The forelegs were short and heavy. Leathery skin on the head and neck was covered with bristly hair and flesh almost completely covered the head, shoulder and hips. The backbone had broken through the animal's side and there was some evidence of decomposition."*

The description of 18-inch (46cm) teeth and "large hind legs" make this particular carcass a real mystery that hasn't been satisfactorily explained.

Bernard Heuvelmans, known as the "father of cryptozoology," mentions an Alaskan incident of a large, rotting carcass in his book *"In The Wake of Sea Serpents."* He dubbed the mass the Shuyak Island Carcass and reported that it washed ashore in July 1951. The carcass was found on the shore of Shuyak Island, north of Kodiak Island at the mouth of the Cook Inlet. Few details were available, but researchers believed the carcass was from some species of whale.

The *London Daily Mail* reported on an Alaskan mystery carcass in its 1957 Yearbook. According to the report, the carcass had washed ashore from the Gulf of Alaska the previous summer. As the news item notes:

"Mystery Monster: A giant hairy Monster, with 6-foot (1.8m) *tusks was washed ashore on the coast of Alaska in July 1956. The carcass which was more than 100 feet* (30.5m) *long and 15 feet*

(4.6m) *wide, had crimson flesh. Its origin and species were a complete mystery. Experts said that it fitted no known description of prehistoric beasts and that the 2-inch* (5.1cm) *reddish-brown hair which covered the thick decaying hide excluded any relationship to whales.*

The Monster was discovered by a veteran Alaskan hunting guide and was apparently washed ashore during a gale in the Gulf of Alaska. Explorers who flew northward to view the carcass, said the Monster had a huge head measuring 5 ½ feet (1.7m) *across, with eye sockets 9 inches* (23cm) *wide and about 42 inches* (107cm) *apart. Its teeth were 6 inches* (15cm) *long and 5 inches* (13cm) *wide at the base. Clusters of ribs extended 6 feet* (1.8m) *from the spinal column, and the moveable upper jaw, a solid tusk-like bone protruded several feet beyond the end of the fixed lower jaw."*

A *United Press* report from the previous year identified the Alaskan guide as Earl Lemming and also included commentary from retired University of Washington zoologist Trevor Kincaid. Kincaid said that, to his knowledge, the description of the carcass didn't fit any prehistoric creature. He further noted that the hair mentioned precluded a connection to a living elephant or whale family member. Kincaid stressed the importance of preserving portions of the carcass for further study and identification. Further details from the UP report included:

"Thick, oily-like blood flowed freely from parts of the flesh when poked with a stick or shovel.

A "flipper" appendage, resembling an elephant's ear, has webbed digits and is about four feet (1.2m) *wide and three feet* (0.9m) *long. The oval upper jaw, with a tusk-like bone, protrudes about 5 feet* (1.5m) *from the end of the fixed lower jaw."*

Initial reports stated the "description fits no known animal." Six months after the discovery, W.A. Clemens, Director of the University of British Columbia's Institute of Oceanography announced his findings, stating the carcass was the remains of a specimen of Baird's Beaked Whale. While the species is common to Alaskan waters, the whales only grow to a maximum length of 42 feet (12.8m), a far cry from the reported 100 feet (30.5m) of the Dry Harbor carcass. No further explanation was ever given, and officials seemed to ignore the discrepancy.

The mystery didn't really go away though. Four years after the find, an article popped up in California's *Pasadena Independent*. The June 15th edition of the paper included commentary from a geologist out of Denver, Colorado who had examined the remains *in situ*. He stated:

"It had a head like that of a baby elephant with a snout. It looked like nothing in the world. Nothing I've ever heard of anywhere."

Why the *Independent* interviewed a geologist for clarity on an unidentified marine animal is as puzzling as the identity of the carcass.

Other assorted globsters were found over the years, usually eventually identified as known marine animals. Another especially odd one turned up in the summer of 2008. It was July 22 when the mystery remains washed up on Nunivak Island, the second largest island in the Bering Sea.

Barry Whitman and his wife Lisa discovered the carcass and on inspection they were positive it wasn't a common animal. As Barry stated:

"I've seen decomposed walrus and whales, and this was just something else."

The Whitmans sent a photo of the creature to Mike Castellini, director of the Coastal Marine Institute at the University of Alaska Fairbanks. Castellini was of the opinion that the carcass was that of a mangled beluga whale with parts of its anatomy somehow obscured.

The photo shows a pinkish-colored carcass with what appears to be a long neck and tail. Cryptozoologist Loren Coleman reported on the discovery in an August 8th, blog post. Coleman notes that locals thought the remains were something out of First Nations legend. According to local lore, a creature called the *Qaqrat* was said to dwell in the area's waters. As Coleman notes:

"At least one resident of Mekoryuk—Nunivak Island's only village—thinks the smooth-skinned corpse might be the lake-dwelling beast rumored about in local legend."

According to native legend, the *Qaqrat*, which translates

as "beast-walrus," left the lake when it dried up and moved into the ocean. It was a walrus-like creature that was never aggressive towards humans.

The Whitman's spotted the carcass while on a salmon fishing trip. From a distance, they thought it was a dead walrus and decided to take a closer look in the event they could salvage the tusks.

They took their skiff close to the shore but couldn't land because of the rocks. They noted a thick coat of hair on the underside of the remains but couldn't distinguish many details of the body. According to Coleman's posting:

"Lisa had the best view. She said the 3-foot (0.9m) *long tail—or what she thinks was the [tail]—seemed to end in a diamond shape. The animal's body was about 6 feet* (1.8m) *long, she said. The head may have been removed or hidden in sand, she said."*

The couple snapped a few photos then left the area to catch up with their fishing partner. They planned to return to the site at a later date, but weather conditions prevented another trip to the spot.

Loren Coleman posted a follow up report on August 27th, which stated:

"The whereabout of the carcass, whether any samples were taken, or even if it has been revisited and bones gathered, are all unknowns."

The carcass, it seems, remains another unsolved mystery.

PART TWO
Sasquatch, Otter Men
& Other Hairy Bipeds

On the trail of the Alaskan sasquatch

Sasquatch in Alaska

Tackling the topic of sasquatch in Alaska is no easy task. First of all, there are the reports, hundreds of them that stretch back to the early days before statehood, up to the present time when the creature is still frequently spotted.

The rich traditions of native Alaskans are filled with stories of hairy men, and with all due respect, I've tried to provide an introduction to some of these perspectives in this volume. It would, quite honestly, be difficult to even write about bigfoot in the state of Alaska without acknowledging the viewpoint of First Nations people. You'll find much of their influence throughout these pages from place names to stories and accounts.

In terms of modern researchers, some excellent work cataloguing Alaskan sightings has been done over the years and for those who are interested, there's a wealth of information to be found. John Green documented some early Alaskan sightings in his work and Loren Coleman, as always, is a great resource for cryptid sightings and information. In particular I'd like to cite the work of J. Robert Alley, whose excellent book *Raincoast Sasquatch* is a treasure trove of accounts. While it also covers Central British Columbia and Northwest Washington, the book is filled with Alaskan reports and provides a good overview of the creature's presence on the northern Pacific coast.

All that being said, it's not my intent to simply replicate the work of these fine gentlemen, although I do quote some of their cases here. The topic of sasquatch in Alaska could easily fill volumes. My intent is to provide a broad picture of the amount of bigfoot activity that occurs in the state from the early days and native legends, to modern reports.

Anyone familiar with the topic of bigfoot is aware of the most famous piece of film of the creature. Known as the

Patterson-Gimlin film, the footage was shot in 1967 in Northern California.

But Daniel Perez, editor and publisher of the *Bigfoot Times* newsletter, reports that the earliest film footage of a sasquatch is from Alaska.

Researcher John Green provided Perez with the information on the account involving a man named Jeffers who captured the brief piece of 8mm film. Green added that the subject was *"... something tall and hairy walking through a field in Alaska."*

Perez had a discussion with Joan Jeffers, who told him her uncle had filmed the clip in Mountain View in 1948.

Apparently, the film is only a few seconds in length and was first viewed by Jeffers in 1991 when he was putting together a video of his family's home movies.

Perez reports on his conversation with Joan Jeffers:

"the film was shot with large electrical towers nearby and that her aunt (Jeffers' aunt) had witnessed the event as her husband shot the film while driving a truck along a road."

Anchorage Press writer Debra McKinney covered the question of sasquatch in Alaska in a March 24, 2016 article. McKinney took a lot of jabs at the field of bigfoot research, at times, pointing out some of the absurdities, but she also spoke to serious researchers.

Michael Thompson of the Alaska Sasquatch Tracker website told McKinney that he's amassed a database with more than 350 accounts stretching back 120 years. Thompson, a customs agent on the Alaska-Yukon border, investigates the accounts when possible. He tells McKinney that some of the sightings are questionable and he's careful what accounts he adds to the ever-growing database:

"A lot of them can be written off, you know, tourists come up here and they've never seen a moose. Then you've got the drugs and alcohol factor. When I go into an interview, you have to prove to me you saw something. Because if I take it at face value, I'd have 20 times the encounters on my website."

Thompson's training as a customs agent gives him an

added advantage in knowing when people are trying to pull the wool over his eyes, but he says pursuing the cryptid isn't always an easy task:

"Some people admire me, and some people think I'm certified crazy, you know, because I do what I do. That's just part of the business, being ridiculed. If you're easily offended, you don't last long in this business."

Like many researchers, Thompson accepts the fact that mainstream science still doesn't believe the creature exist, but he notes that, at the least, the amount of data makes it a fascinating topic worth studying:

"...given the number of sightings and encounters from people of all walks of life, from ditch diggers on up to doctors and lawyers, there's surely something out there that's evading people, and it's worth looking into. Even if it's proven to be a complete hoax, you still have centuries and centuries of folklore, and that's worth studying."

Worth studying indeed. More and more, people are interested in the creatures lurking in the vast wilds of Alaska. As we shall see, those creatures often make themselves known, and as researchers continue to collect information and accounts, perhaps the last frontier will provide some interesting answers to the sasquatch question.

Alaskan native group 1800s

Alaskan First Nations & the Hairy Men

Alaska has a greater concentration of indigenous people than any other state in the union, and the federal government currently recognizes 227 tribes in the state. Aleuts, Athabascans, Haida, Inupiat, Tlingit and Yuit make up the state's major groups.

Unlike the lower 48 states, native tribes in Alaska are not organized on reservations but rather in villages. Of course, many First Nations people also live in the various cities and towns around the state.

The topic of Native Alaskans and their perspective of what we call bigfoot is a very complex one. Views of the creatures are often wrapped in spiritual concepts that don't always translate easily to the English language, and even when they do, the cultural and spiritual foundation of the people must be understood in order to grasp the full concept.

There are 20 recognized native languages in Alaska that fall into four language families. With so many tribes and so many languages, even the names used for bigfoot vary widely. Among these terms are *Arulataq, Ahoolahuk, Get'qun* and *Nant'ina* to name but a few. Often these terms translate roughly to "hairy man" like the Eskimo word "*Urayuli.*" In other cases, the translations are even more difficult.

Concepts like the *Kushtaka*, discussed later, are even more confusing for non-natives to understand since they border on sasquatch-like tales, yet are considered completely different by Alaskan natives.

It's also common to hear English terms used to describe the creatures. Beyond the commonly known bigfoot and sasquatch, other used terms include the woodsman, the bushman and the big man.

Despite the language barriers, general descriptions of the creatures are very similar across the state. They are described as averaging at least six to seven feet (1.8–2.4m) tall and sometimes as tall as ten feet (3.1m). They are covered in brown, black or red hair. The face is humanlike with recognizable features.

The arms are long, reaching to the knees, and the creatures move in large strides, covering much more ground at a faster pace than any human can move. Many stories say an awful smell accompanies the creatures, and they are known to emit an unearthly scream as well as other unusual noises.

In his book, *Make Prayers to the Raven: A Koyukon View of the Northern Forest*, Richard K. Nelson remarks on the nature of what he calls the woodsman:

"It is as real as any other creature in the vast Koyukon wildland, but far more mysterious. It is always there, somewhere, but almost never seen. It is an incongruous sound in the distance, a movement just beyond the thicket, a diabolical laugh in the darkness. It is something unaccountably thrown toward a lonely hunter, meat that vanishes in the night from drying racks, something stolen from an unattended camp, a child gone without a trace. It is called nuhu'anh (also nik'inla'eena or nik'il'eena), 'it sneaks here and there.' And in English it is named woodsman."

Traditionally, First Nations people have been reluctant to speak to many outsiders about the hairy men. There are a variety of reasons for this, including doubt that non-natives will understand, fear of ridicule and cultural taboos regarding the discussion of some topics. But there's also another factor. Many native Alaskan groups are protective of the hairy men. It's believed they serve a specific purpose and that, for the most part, they should be left alone to live in the wild in peace.

As Richard K. Nelson notes, some natives believe the connection between humans and the hairy men is even closer than westerners commonly consider, calling them, essentially, humans in another form:

"The distinction between humans and animals is further blurred by recognition of a human creature that occupies the wildlands and

remains almost totally alien from society. This is nik'inla'eena, 'the sneaker,' called 'woodsman' in English. Woodsmen are as real as any other inhabitant of the Koyukon environment, but they are extremely shy and quick to vanish when people come near. They are said to be human who became wild either after committing murder or engaging in cannibalism. Occasionally they harass people or steal from them, but they are not a great danger. People tell countless stories about encounters with woodsmen and regard them as regular inhabitants of the environment. They are especially interesting as a bridge across the narrow gap between humans and animals or between the worlds of humanity and nature."

Native artist Silyas Saunders from Bella Coola says he saw one of the creatures when he was a child in the 1940s. From his perspective, the hairy men are strange, supernatural creatures:

"We learned growing up that the creature has supernatural powers. They can transform into spirits and have super-lightning speed. People see them all the time, but nobody knows where they make their homes."

Naturally, there are exceptions to these views and in recent years, there have been First Nations people who have begun collecting tales of the big men to make sure the traditions and beliefs are not lost in the modern era. In some cases, there are native researchers who have joined to quest to prove the existence of bigfoot, coming to the belief that the creatures are an undiscovered species.

Storyteller John Active has amassed a collection of accounts of the *Urayuli* from the Yup'ik people of Southwest Alaska. Active, a Yup'ik himself from Bethel, says the *Urayuli* is often described as ten feet (3m) tall, covered with hair, and having glowing eyes.

According to tribal lore, children who become lost in the woods are transformed into *Urayuli*.

It's said to wander the frozen tundra and cries out in loneliness with a voice resembling a loon. While the creature is often frightening, the *Urayuli* doesn't directly harm people.

In appearance it is said to look very much like the traditional image of a bigfoot, standing 7 to 10 feet (2.1 – 3m) tall, sometimes as tall as 14 feet (4.3m), and covered with shaggy hair, its features said to be very apelike. However, the *Urayuli* has glowing red eyes and freakishly long arms that reach down to its ankles. The beast is allegedly very adept at swimming and has been blamed for stealing livestock and pets over the years, as well as raiding campsites or stealing fish from fishermen. Alleged tracks of the *Urayuli* have been sporadically found, almost always near water, and there was even a supposed photograph of one standing on a mountain ridge taken by a hunting guide in 1982 near the city of Dillingham.

A passage from *Living with Wildness* tells of a Yup'ik elder's encounter with a hairy man:

"John Gumlickpuk, a Yup'ik elder, once encountered a Hairy Man near Togiak. Then in his early thirties, he went outside at sunrise and met a man covered with long hair. 'He was as big as us, but hairy all over,' Gumlickpuk recounted. 'The only place he didn't have hair was his face.'

Startled by Gumlickpuk, the man quickly ran away, Speedy exits are characteristic of many Bristol Bay Hairy Men, who by most accounts can run incredibly fast. They can also jump high and far, sometimes over rivers or trees. Case in point: John Gumlickpuk's wife, Elena, tells of a Hairy Man who was spotted by a woman washing clothes. When confronted, she says, 'He jump off, way far. He could jump over high bushes and really run fast.'"

The Gwich'in are an Athabascan tribe of the far north. They speak of the *"Na'in,"* or "brushman," another dangerous version of the hairy beast that lives in the Alaskan wilderness. The *Na'in* are said to have been humans who were shunned by the people for violations of tribal law. They took to the wilderness and became something more than ordinary men.

The *Na'in* have strange powers, including the ability to exert mind control over humans and the power to cause people to fall asleep. They are said to utilize these abilities to abduct people, often women, for companionship.

Other Athabascan people in Alaska tell similar tales of strange creatures that steal women from villages. Bob Attla, brother of dog-mushing legend George Attla, recounted a Hairy

Man story he learned from his father.

Reportedly, in the late 1920s, a woman vanished from a village in the Huslia area. No trace of her could be found and the tribe was unable to locate her. Several years later, a group of hunters looking for game spotted a woman out on the tundra. They recognized her as the woman who had vanished years previously. They called out to get her attention, but when she spotted them, she ran away.

When the hunters caught up with the woman, they were able to speak with her. She told them she had been living with the Hairy Man. She told the villagers she liked him and wanted to stay with him. She also pleaded with the hunters not to shoot the Hairy Man if they saw him.

The hunters released the woman and shared the story with the rest of the villagers. Over the years, the woman was seen periodically but always kept her distance.

Sometimes the people themselves sent companions out for the Hairy Men. Legends from Aliknigik, north of Dillingham, say the creatures lived north of the village for many years. Purportedly, in the old days, villagers would take a young woman to the area and leave her there for the Hairy Man. As long as they did this periodically, the wild men would not harass the village or the people.

Many native people say the Hairy Men aren't dangerous, but they can bring trouble. As Nelson states regarding the woodsmen:

"Woodsmen are mainly regarded as a nuisance rather than a serious threat. They often steal meat, fish, and other things from summer camps, and they harass people by whistling, throwing sticks, or making evil-sounding laughter nearby. I was told that 'a woodsman will play tricks on people too, if it's a playful one—like stretching somebody's fishnet out in the trees.'"

Rock throwing is also a frequent occurrence, though it isn't always aggressive. At times it may be a warning, or a message to leave the area.

An elder in St. Mary's said that she and her husband had

rocks thrown at them from the brush along the riverbank while they were traveling by boat up the Andreafsky River. The rock throwers remained hidden so there were no clear sightings, however, the couple knew they were the *"Miluquyulit"* or, "the ones who throw things."

According to the elders, the hairy creatures are a part of the Earth's biology because only a "natural being" would be capable of picking up rocks that large and throwing them.

In some parts of Alaska, the creatures are known as the *Tornit*, or the bushman.

According to the 1901 edition of the *Bulletin of the American Museum of Natural History*, Volume 15, the Alaskan *"Tornit"* are described thusly:

"In early times the Tornit, a race of very large people, inhabited the country. They quarreled with the Eskimo because the latter intruded upon their land. This made the Tornit angry, who broke the ground with their lances and spears, and split rocks into pieces."

The bulletin article states that the giants would often wait for village men to leave for a hunt. With the community unprotected, the *Tornits* would raid the village.

According to the 1901 Bulletin, *"It is said that in the Iglulik country the land still shows how the Tornit tore it up with their harpoon-shafts when they were about to leave, in fear of the Eskimo."*

Terrye Tombs, writing for the *Anchorage Daily News*, states that the *Tornits* originally came across the Bering Land Bridge.

"In the beginning, the story goes, the Inuit and the tornits lived peacefully in villages near each other and shared common hunting grounds.

The Inuit people often built and used kayaks for hunting. While the tornits were unable to master the building of kayaks, they were very aware of the advantages of having and using one. One story goes that a young tornit borrowed a young Inuit's kayak without permission and damaged the bottom of it. The young Inuit became very angry and stabbed the tornit in the nape of the neck while he was sleeping, killing him. The rest of the tornits feared that they too, would be killed by the Inuit and fled the country, rarely to be seen again"

Toombs has her own story involving a *Tornit* sighting. While on a salmon fishing trip in the Deshka and Little Sustina rivers on a cool and rainy Spring day, Terrye and her brother noticed a foul odor and alerted their father.

Toombs' father noticed that most of the other fishermen had already left the area and quickly followed suit. When his children asked why they were leaving, the man replied that a bear was nearby. Terrye recalled seeing uprooted trees in the area that had been thrust into the ground.

"'I learned many years later that that was a tell-tale sign of bigfoot territory,' Toombs wrote. 'I guess I'll never know if that was a bear or a bigfoot that displaced us from fishing that evening, but I do know, that was the last time our families ever fished that river. It was also the first and only time all the kids got to sleep (or at least tried to) in the camp trailer instead of the tents.'"

Sasquatch display in downtown Anchorage

Bethel Encounters

The city of Bethel is the largest community on the Kuskokwim River and is the ninth largest community in the state with a population of over 6,000 people. More than half of the residents are native Alaskans.

The original residents of what became Bethel were the Mamterillermiut, or, "Smokehouse People."

Bethel has been an active area for sasquatch sightings over the years, from early native tales to modern accounts, the creature has crept around the region for decades.

One early account is the legend of a young boy who turned into a Hairy Man. *The Delta Discovery* mentions the tale in a 2013 article:

"Here in the Bethel area, many people's introduction to Hairy Man was through the creature we came to know of as 'Gabriel Fox' in the 1960s. It's the story of a young boy who ran away from the Children's Home near Kwethluk and survived in the wilderness by turning into a Hairy Man.

But big questions remain: How could a boy turn into a hairy creature that lived in the extreme wild? Was it really Gabriel Fox, and not a young Bigfoot that was starving and raiding fish camps for food when it was caught? Why did the military and/or the US government say nothing about him after they took him away? And most importantly, why didn't they return him home?"

Unfortunately, there aren't a lot of details available about the Gabriel Fox tale, but sightings of bigfoot continue to be reported in the Bethel area. Here are a few highlights of the area's many sightings:

A pair of fishermen checking their nets at the upper mouth of the Tarpernaq River spotted a bigfoot in August 2011.

The men, Dana Kopanuk and his nephew Paul Fisher, had gone up the river from Bethel looking for whitefish. When they reached the end of Napaskiak Slough (also known as Tarpernaq Slough) they set their net at the mouth of a small eddy. They left the area and returned three hours later to check their net before heading home.

When they returned to the area, they saw a figure in the trees near the bank. They assumed it was someone from a nearby fish camp, so they paid little mind at first, but they soon noticed unusual features. The figure was gray in color and walking slowly. Kopanuk reports:

"It looked like it had not much of a neck. It looked like a huge person. The willows were tall, but it was taller. If it were a person, he would have waited for us. But it didn't, it just kept walking away..."

The men watched the figure for about five minutes until it vanished into the trees. In later conversation, the men both agreed that the figure wasn't human. On seeing drawings of bigfoot, Kopanuk stated it matched the figure that they had seen.

Passengers in a bush plane headed to Bethel spotted a pair of creatures running on the ice in May 2012.

The plane was following the Kuskokwim River. While much of the snow had melted in the area, ice on the river was still breaking up.

As the plane passed over Tuluksak, a passenger spotted something on the ice below. Looking closely, he observed two bipedal forms on the frozen water. One of the figures was large in size, the other small. Both were dark in color and could be seen clearly since they were running on pure white ice. The creatures appeared to be running from the sound of the airplane.

The man pointed the figures out to the pilot who couldn't see them clearly. He turned the plane at an angle to get a better look and was able to spot one of the creatures himself. One of the figures appeared to be holding something close to its chest and the pair was running side by side.

The man had the impression the figures were a parent and

its offspring. They seemed to be running for the shoreline, likely to get into the nearby forest.

The pilot turned the plane toward the figures causing them to jump into the ring of melt water. According to the witness' report, the larger creature went in first followed by the second smaller figure.

"They caused a large wake or ring of water to spread out on top of the water," the man stated.

The pilot circled the spot a few times waiting for the creatures to resurface. When they didn't the man turned the plane and kept going.

A Bethel family picking berries on August 3, 2013 spotted a large, black hairy creature near the village of Napakiak.

The family of three, a mother, father and their young daughter, were out along the Pengug River when they spotted the bigfoot. The hairy man was walking along the Napakiak-Atmautluak Trail when the father spotted it and pointed it out to his wife.

As the couple were watching the creature, an airplane flew overhead. The sound startled the bigfoot and it crouched down as the plane passed over the area. It then stood and walked down a rise in the tundra.

The sighting occurred at about 6:30 in the evening, shortly before a torrential rainstorm hit the area.

Wild Men & Vicious Bushmen

Wild Men made frequent appearances in American newspapers in the 1800s. Due to the questionable reporting of the period, it's not always easy to tell whether the stories are truth, only partial fact, or complete fabrication.

On some occasions, stories were a blend of fact and folklore. No doubt, those sitting around telling campfire stories took liberties with real incidents, making them more exciting with the addition of Wild Men and other monsters.

Case in point, one of the stories involving the Nahanni Monster.

Stories about the beast arose during the Klondike boom between the late 1890s and early 1900s. Old time prospectors in the Juneau area claimed the Wild Man was on the loose in the country and was viciously killing miners.

Legend says one group of men failed to return to Wrangell for supplies and a search party was sent out to find them. They found the missing prospector's camp along the Nahanni river 300 miles (483km) northeast of Wrangell. The scene at the camp was disturbing. The miners were all dead, their bodies had been torn to pieces, and partially devoured. There were no signs of bears or wolves in the area, but giant, manlike footprints were found around the campsite. Searchers reported that the miners had been killed by a "wild man."

Locals said the Nahanni Monster was a giant capable of tearing a normal-sized human limb from limb.

There are plenty of fantastic stories from the Alaskan frontier that remain unexplained, but the truth of the Nahanni Monster is much more human than animal.

The real story involves two men named McLeod who were

found dead at their camp on the south banks of the Nahanni River. The men had not been dismembered or eaten though; their deaths were due to gunshot wounds.

Official reports made no mention of giant footprints or any other signs of an unknown giant, wild man, or other creature.

There are minor accounts from the early 1900s that claim wild men, and sometimes wild women, were in the Wrangell area and that witnesses had heard them speaking an unknown language. One brief account come from 1918 when a German prospector purportedly had an encounter. The man was traveling from a northern mining camp, trying to make his way back to the town of Wrangell.

While searching for food and provisions, the man fell asleep and was awoken by talking nearby. Excited at the prospect of having company in the wild, he went around some high bramble looking for the source of the voice he heard.

To his shock, he discovered a "bushwoman" sitting on the ground feeding berries to a small hairy child. The man claimed the hairy creature was speaking in an "Indian language."

The *Fairbanks Daily News-Miner.* out of Fairbanks Alaska, reported on a string of wild man incidents in the 1930s. An article from 1931 gives an update on the sightings:

"Latest word in Fairbanks about the 'wild man' of Nation River, along the Yukon, comes from Fred Glendenning who returned to the city a few days ago. The 'wild man' who is rapidly becoming a legend, lives alone, and has never seen many of his fellow men. His clothes, it is reported, are made of animal skins; he lives in caves and the marks of his bare feet, almost resembling those of a wild beast, have been spotted on beaches. It is said that the man enters cabins to take ammunition and has been known to burn the houses for no apparent reason.

Some say he is merely a myth, and that his story began six or seven years ago when white trappers wanted to keep Indians out of that section of the country."

Later news accounts implied the culprit being described as a wild man was one Albert Johnson, an outlaw who had killed a mounted policeman and evaded authorities by hiding out in the Alaskan wilderness.

There's no doubt Johnson was responsible for some of the accounts attributed to wild man activity, but the interesting aspect was the reaction of local Alaskan natives who were cautious of the legendary wild man or hairy creature they claimed had long lurked in the area.

As the original stories stated, mere talk of the wild man was enough to keep natives out of the region. The area is in what is now the Yukon-Charley Rivers National Preserve, not far from the state's border with the Yukon Territory.

Just a few years later, on the other side of the state, a wild man was reportedly running around Bristol Bay. Dubbed "The wild man of the Nashagak," locals had known about him for years. In its January 19, 1935 edition, Newark's *Ohio Advocate* reports:

"Anchorage, Alaska, Jan 19—(AP)—Out of the isolated district north of Bristol Bay comes a tale of 'the wild man of the Nashagak'—a nebulous terror jealously guarding an empire which, even on the larger maps, is an unexplored white patch with dotted lines for streams.

Charles J. Dumbolton, sourdough prospector of many years in Yukon and Klondike valley camps, told the story today after arriving by plane from a season of prospecting 125 miles (201km) from the nearest settlement.

The wild man is believed in so firmly by the few men in the area, that they have drawn a voluntary boundary to their northern trips. While he has made no effort to investigate the wild man's authenticity, Dumbolton said he found trappers feared to venture beyond their own established frontier, the King Salmon river.

He said the wild man, perhaps some man crazed by loneliness, has been reported seen several times, and is blamed for the disappearance of several men who have ventured into the region of the upper Nashgak and its tributaries during the last several seasons.

The wild man's empire is a vast region between the south-flowing Upper Nashgak and the westward-flowing middle course of the Kuskowim."

Bushmen

Often called the bushman, or woodsman in early accounts, the hairy giants weren't always prone to vanishing in the woods in Alaska. Sometimes, they were aggressive.

Take the case of Albert Petka. Petka lived on a boat on the Yukon River near Nulato, a small fishing village. The village had long been inhabited by native Athabascans, prospectors and Russian fur traders.

Reportedly, in the 1920s, Petka was attacked by a hairy giant, though there are variations as to the exact details of the encounter. Some accounts claim the conflict took place on board Petka's boat; other versions say the man was on shore when he met the creature.

What is consistent, is that Petka had dogs with him when he came across the hairy creature. During the conflict, the man's dogs were able to drive the creature away. The man told other people about the conflict, but he died as a result of the injuries inflicted on him by the beast.

Given the time period and the location, details of the report have been difficult to verify. Reportedly, there was another fatal conflict with a bushman in 1943.

John Mire, known in the area as "The Dutchman," was assaulted by a creature close to DeWilde's Camp near Yuki Island, downriver from the town of Ruby.

Mire fought with the creature but was able to make his escape and get to his boat. He piloted the craft to a nearby settlement to get help, telling people about his encounter before he died from his wounds.

Just as in the Petka tale, Mire's dogs purportedly drove the creature away.

The similarities between the tales imply the accounts may be one in the same though they are 23 years apart. There are few details available in either case and we are left to wonder whether or not the tales are mere legend or whether they have some grain of truth.

John Green was doubtful that the accounts were genuine,

pointing out that there should have been more publicity about the incidents, even on the frontier.

"...if such a creature decided to attack a man, I find it strangely coincidental that in each case the man should have survived temporarily with facial injuries, or that the dogs should have conveniently driven it off. However, there is certainly nothing impossible in the incidents described."

Whatever the reality, there are other reports of the bushman along the river, especially between the towns of Ruby and Nulato, and natives of the region have long believed the creatures dwell in the area.

Another legend of a violent encounter with a hairy giant comes from the 1960s and involves a miner from Nome. In this case, the human came out on the winning side of the confrontation.

According to the tale, the miner, a man named Jean Joiner, owned a mine near Jade Mountain on Dahl Creek. Jade Mountain is along the Kobuk River near the small towns of Ambler and Shungnak. Joiner was mining green jade, Alaska's state gem, from the mountains.

Details of the story are scant, but it seems Joiner spotted a large animal near his mine. He thought the creature was a bear, so he shot and killed it but when he examined the body, he discovered it had human features.

Joiner was frightened that he had killed a person and believed the authorities would come after him. Reportedly, he cut the body into pieces and threw them all into a stream near his home.

He eventually told a group of people about the incident, one of which was a BLM representative from Nome.

Supposedly, in 1966, another miner in the Dahl Creek area found large, manlike tracks around his camp. He later spotted an enormous creature walking on two legs. Although he took some shots at the thing, he didn't kill it or even hit it.

The slim details of this account imply that it's either a version of the Joiner tale, or perhaps even the real, original account. Whatever the case, the truth of the story remains obscured in the cold snows of northern Alaska.

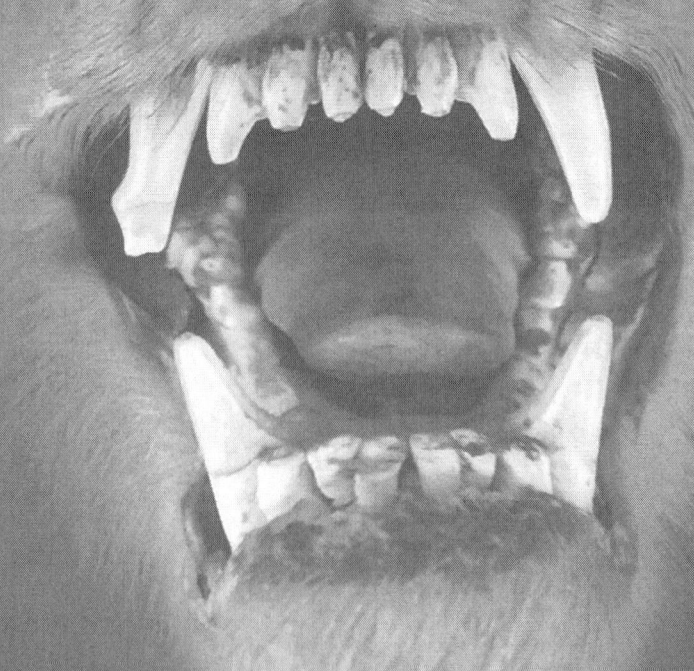

NUNIVAK
ISLAND

Decades of Sightings

1930s-1950s

Nunivak is a permafrost-covered volcanic island about thirty miles offshore from the delta of the Yukon and Kuskokwim rivers. It's the second largest island in the Bering Sea and has only one community, Mekoryuk. According to the 2010 census, the community only has 191 residents. The entire population of the island lives in Mekoryuk, which is situated on the north coast of the island.

One winter in the 1930s, Fred Weston Sr. and two other men made their way to the west side of the island in search of game. Nunivak has a population of reindeer and musk oxen, and the men were looking to stock up their food supply by doing some hunting.

They stopped at an old fishcamp and chose one of the abandoned buildings as a shelter for the night. The building, an old sod house, had a small entryway but would be a good spot to keep warm. The men had been traveling by dog teams, and before bedding down for the evening, they secured the animals to wooden posts outside the building.

Before they were asleep, the men were alerted by the wild barking of their dogs. The next moment, someone, or something, was trying to break through the door of the building.

The shaken men grabbed their rifles and stood at the ready, prepared to fire at whatever might burst through the door. According to the account, "whatever was trying to enter the sod house was too big to fit through the doorway."

They stopped at an old fishcamp and chose one of the abandoned buildings as a shelter for the night. The building, an old sod house, had a small entryway but would be a good spot to keep warm. The men had been traveling by dog teams, and before bedding down for the evening, they secured the animals to wooden posts outside the building.

Before they were asleep, the men were alerted by the wild barking of their dogs. The next moment, someone, or something, was trying to break through the door of the building.

The shaken men grabbed their rifles and stood at the ready, prepared to fire at whatever might burst through the door. According to the account, "whatever was trying to enter the sod house was too big to fit through the doorway."

The assault on the door stopped and the men heard something walking away from the house. They ventured out to see the culprit and spotted a *"tall, silvery-colored creature, walking upright and away from the old fishcamp into the distance. It soon disappeared from view behind a hill."*

There are also some scattered reports of Sasquatch sightings from the 1940s and 1950s.

Legendary bigfoot hunter, Californian Bob Titmus, reportedly saw one of the creatures during WWII. Titmus was going to Alaska on a small ship in May, 1942. Titmus went on deck late one evening and saw *"...on the beach close at hand an erect creature about seven feet* (2.1m) *high covered with dark hair and very heavy."*

John Green reports that Titmus' sighting likely occurred in the Wrangell Narrows and that Titmus didn't *"really credit what he had seen."*

Although the sighting is only a footnote, it likely had more bearing years later when Titmus was actively searching for the creature.

A sighting from 1951 or 1952 has a few more details. The account was reported by Mr. R.B., a demolition professional from Ketchikan. The incident occurred when the witness was a boy and took place on Prince of Wales Island.

"I was working with my grandfather on our thirty-six-foot fishing boat, the Verna May, somewhere on Prince of Wales Island. I don't remember the exact location, but I do remember us anchoring up

close to shore one nice evening and going to bed. It was after midnight, and I had got up to go on deck, as we had no facilities inside in the cabin. As I flipped open the cabin door onto the deck, I felt the boat rock, and right in front of me, in my flashlight beam was this tall, hair-covered, manlike creature, climbing up over the side of the boat, all wet. He was dark brown or black. As soon as he saw me, he just kicked off backwards into the water with a big splash. Granddad came up quick and looked with me, but it wasn't' swimming on the surface anywhere. Then, just a few seconds later, we could see this seven-or eight-foot (2.1 - 2.4m)figure stand up out of the shallows about forty yards (37m) away. It stood up on two legs and walked straight up into the forest. It sure covered that distance underwaters fast! Granddad saw it stand up too, and he got real scared. He pulled the anchor and started the engine right away and we got out of there. We kept moving for a time until we got to another anchorage late that night. In almost fifty years on the water and in the bush that was the only time I seen one of those things!"

An Aleut elder, Ted Angasan, told writer Bill Sherwonit that a friend of his had seen a hairy man in the village of South Naknek in the late 1950s. The young man, Peter, saw the creature laying on some 55-gallon (208 liter) fuel drums. The hairy man was shocked and so was Peter. As Sherwonit relates:

"Peter grabbed his gun, shot—and missed. The creature, in turn, screamed loudly, and then took off running.

Peter ran too, and didn't stop until he reached the village, where he told of his meeting with Hairy Man. Most people remained skeptical. 'They though he'd seen everything but a Hairy Man,' Angasan recalled. 'But I believed. You can tell when a guy is lying or not. He was scared to death.'"

In August 1956, another Californian spotted a sasquatch near the southern tip of the panhandle of the inside passage. Bob Everett of Santa Barbara was on the deck of a fishing boat anchored north of Ketchikan when he spotted the hairy creature. The ship was anchored for the night, but I've found no further details of the incident.

Another sighting of a bigfoot occurred the same year. This time the witness was fishing fifty miles southwest of Ketchikan when he saw the thing. He estimated its height at about eight feet (2.4m) and thought it weighed about 400 pounds (181 kilos). The creature was walking on two legs when he observed it.

Traveling Alaskan backroads

1960s - 1970s

A few years after Everett's sighting, a young man had an encounter in the same area. It was 1960 and the lad had gone out to haul in a skiff. He left a flashlight pointing towards the shore so he could see what he was doing. Looking up, he spied a large, human-like figure standing waist deep in the water between the float and the shore.

The boy reported that the thing was *"...not exactly a person but had arms and head like a man."*

The creature was grayish white and had *"Big, round beady eyes."* The boy screamed out for help and a group of men came rushing to the area. When more lights hit the creature, it dove under water and swam away like a frog.

Several reports from the 1960s claimed a sasquatch was active in the woods around the small village of Galena in Alaska's interior. Residents said the thing was quick on its feet and quickly ran away each time someone tried to get a clear look at it.

A Ketchikan man described seeing a creature in the Wrangell-Petersburg area in the late summer of 1960. Robert Alley lists the man as Paul M., an electrician, and gives his brief account:

"I had been camped out on a fishing trip near the mouth of Ohmer Creek, eighteen miles (29km) south of Petersburg by road, near Blind Slough, and had been near my tent by the creek after dark, when I heard splashing just a few yards up by Ohmer Creek. I shone my flashlight level, and very close to me, just a few yards away, were two long, hair-covered legs, brownish in color. They were a lot longer than a bear's. I could just make out a large body above but didn't' shine the light up in the direction of the head. Instead, I just decided to turn and head for my car! I didn't see it again after that."

In the 1960s, Bob Titmus was actively searching for sasquatch in the Pacific Northwest. He discovered a set of tracks on a small island in Alaska in the fall of 1961. The exact location of the find is not given. Titmus detailed the discovery in a letter to monster hunter Tom Slick:

"When I started out that day the weather and water wasn't too awfully bad; but a couple of hours later a first-class storm suddenly bore down on me from the west. The wind was blowing so hard and the seas running so high that I didn't dare turn broadside to it and run for a bay a couple of miles up ahead. I continued burrowing almost straight into it and made for a couple of small islands less than a mile ahead.

I had been on these islands before and knew that they were joined by a large sandbar, inhabited with clams, which seemed a nice little bay that was a good anchorage, especially if the tide wasn't too high.

That was a long trip. The dinghy was in tow and was soon swamped. One seat and both oars were carried away; this being the second set of oars to be lost in a month. Upon arrival at the little bay you should have seen the inside of that boat! It looked like—well, it was just scrambled, everything awash in a large portion of the ocean that had come aboard. The waves were breaking wild over the sandbar and I wasn't even certain whether the tide was on the rise or fall.

The anchor seemed to be holding alright for the moment at least so I went below to clean up the mess. When this was finished, I climbed atop the cabin for a look at the water and weather outside past the bar. It seemed to be quieting down just a little. It was while I was standing up there that I scanned the sandy beach on the island to the right and saw this string of large tracks with a long stride. I felt certain that these were what we've been looking for and an inspection with the binoculars confirmed it.

Although I was little more than a hundred feet (30m) off the island there seemed no way to get ashore without swimming; --eventually I screwed up my courage, stripped off and did just that. The tracks came out of the water angling toward the timber and the undergrowth, paralleled the growth line for about 125 feet (38m) and then entered it. The tracks would measure about 13 or 13 ½ inches (33 – 34cm) long and were approximately 6 inches (15cm) wide at the ball of the foot. The stride would have been just about an even four feet (1.2m). Some of the impressions were quite deep although the creature was only walking. It would be impossible to estimate with any degree of accuracy the age of the tracks since it was raining hard at the time and had been more or less steadily for days one end. Nor was there any clue offered where the tracks abruptly started at what had been a tide line. From what was left of the impressions and for all practical purposes I would say that these tracks were very similar to the fourteen-inch (36cm) track that we are familiar with in California.

I did not find any other tracks on the beach of this island nor where he made his exit from the trees. Was not too successful in following these tracks in the undergrowth; however, I must confess I did not spend any great amount of time on the island as I was literally turning blue with cold and was in constant fear that the boat would pull its anchor and be carried away. Needless to say, there were no measurements, casts or photos taken."

Russell "Rusty" Annabel was a colorful and controversial character born in Tacoma, Washington in 1904. Rusty moved to Alaska as a teenager and became a notable figure. He was considered one of the best outdoor writers of the period, publishing mainly in *Sports Afield Magazine*.

The July 1963 issue of the magazine published a piece by Annabel detailing one of his adventures with another legendary Alaskan outdoorsman, Tex Cobb.

Early in his career, Annabel had connected with Cobb and the two heard native tales of a "man-eating giant" known as the *Gilyuk*.

According to Annabel, Cobb had frequent encounters with Alaska's native tribes and had an understanding with them:

"No sentiment was wasted on either side, but he and the tribesmen had a live-and-let-live understanding that was rare in those days…due to the fact that the Indians trusted him, we became involved one autumn with what would be called, I suppose, an abominable snowman."

Annabel writes that he later learned more about the legendary Tibetan monster, including seeing photographs of tracks taken in the Himalayan mountains. The similarity between the Himalayan tales and things he had learned about the *Gilyuk* in Alaska led him to think the two were similar.

As he reported in the *Sports Afield* article:

"…when I was a youngster roaming the North with Tex, we had never heard much about Gilyuk, the shaggy cannibal giant sometimes called The-Big-Man-with-The-Little-Hat.

Our adventure with Gilyuk occurred while we were camped in a pretty spruce park on Yellowjacket Creek, south of Tyone Lake. We had spent the entire summer on this mountain girt Nelchina Plateau, wandering and looking for fur sign.

Maybe we were. He always had to have an excuse for enjoying the country, a commercial excuse if he could think of one. Anyway, it was now late September, the beautiful time, no mosquitoes, the land ablaze with color, the fish and the meat animals' summer-fat, the caribou horde gathering, and we were footloose and free as perhaps men can never be again."

A group of six natives appeared in Cobb and Annabel's

camp that morning. Cobb asked the men if they had eaten and they said they had. Clearly, something had disturbed the men and in short order, Cobb and Annabel discovered what the problem was. The group's leader, a man referred to as "Chief Stickman," was familiar to Annabel and proceeded to tell the two frontiersmen that he had trouble.

"He had come into this area two days ago, he said, with some of his people to kill and cache caribou for winter use. But they discovered that Gilyuk, the shaggy giant, was hanging around. They had found sign yesterday. And of course, everybody knew that Gilyuk wasn't interested in caribou. Gilyuk ate men.

'What kind of sign?' Tex asked.

'We will take you to see it,' Stickman said, 'It is not far.'

After breakfast we followed the Indians upstream a couple of miles to a burned flat on which a nurse crop of aspen and birch had grown. In the center of the flat stood a ruined birch sapling. It had been about four inches (10cm) through and maybe ten feet (3m) tall. Something had twisted the sapling as a man would twist a matchstick. The wood had separated into individual fibers, the bark hung in tatters. Stickman and his hunters stood back, while Tex and I looked the site over. Moose often ride a sapling down to get at the tender upper twigs. So do caribou. But no moose or caribou had done this. This had been done by something with hands. It had happened yesterday, because the leaves of the sapling had not yet completely wilted.

It wasn't the work of lightning—no burns. A freak whirlwind hadn't done it, because trees and brush a few yards distant were undamaged. The hard ground showed no tracks. We found no snagged hair in the brush. Absolutely nothing except the incredibly twisted birch sapling. It was without question the eeriest sight I ever beheld in the wilds.

Stickman said, 'It is Gilyuk's mark. We have seen it before.'"

Stickman proceeded to ask Cobb and Annabel if they would camp with his men until the caribou hunt was completed. "Gilyuk doesn't molest white men. Perhaps he will not molest us if you are in camp," Stickman told the pair.

Cobb agreed to move camp the next morning and join the

band at their location, a spot about two hours east.

According to Annabel, Chief Stickman was later killed by the *Gilyuk*. Reports claimed the man had gotten up one night and went down to the lake, perhaps for a drink of water. But the *Gilyuk* struck and took the man. A portion of his clothing was found by the river and showed signs of having been torn off the man. A search party failed to find anything more, and even Tex Cobb was convinced the old chief had been killed by the *Gilyuk*.

Annabel was known to exaggerate at times, so how far he stretched the truth in this particular tale is anyone's guess.

In *The Field Guide to Bigfoot, Yeti, and Other Mystery Primates Worldwide*, Loren Coleman and Patrick Huyghe list the "Gilyuk" as an alternative name for a true giant. They write:

"True Giants occasionally wear primitive clothing, especially in colder climates..."

Some researchers speculate that the concept of the "little hat" arose due to the pointed head often attributed to bigfoot-like creatures. The point is believed to be a sagittal crest, a ridge of bone that runs lengthwise along the midline top of the skull. From a distance, the sagittal crest could give the impression that the creature was wearing a small hat on its oversized head.

In 1964, a man hunting about 35 miles (56km) south of Fairbanks saw a sasquatch and quickly retreated because he believed the creature wasn't alone. He wasn't someone who put stock into reports of the creatures until he had his own sighting. As he recalls:

"...something that I would not believe unless I saw it. It just stepped up about thirty feet (9.1m) in front of me, stared at me, kind of grunted and walked into the woods real quietly."

The witness was out hunting so he was armed, though he states he didn't feel threatened. Nevertheless, the man did elect to get out of the area and headed back to his vehicle.

He described the creature as at least six feet (1.8m) tall with shaggy, dark brown hair. When the beast went into the woods, it seemed to start communicating with others of its kind. As the witness states:

"I headed back to my car, often glancing over my shoulder, I heard cracking branches and low-to-high tones coming from the direction (it) went. What made me walk a little faster was that those sounds were answered from the other side of the road."

Bob Titmus was in Alaska when another incident occurred in July 1965. The encounter involved a man who lived in Butedale, a small town on a large island that faces the mainland across a narrow channel of the Inside Passage. At the time, the town had few year-round residents.

The man in question was a shore worker but owned his own small boat and fished for recreation. He and a friend often went out fishing together, and on the occasion of the encounter, they had left home at different times, each taking their own boat.

John Green describes the incident in *Sasquatch: the Apes Among Us*:

"...there is a small island in front of the village. The place where they fished was near the mainland shore on the far side of the small island. On this occasion the first man stopped his motor when he noticed something in the shadows on a tiny islet about 75 yards (68.6m) away and something else in the water. They were well worth a second look. On the islet were two gigantic bipedal creatures, very dark in color, very heavily built and covered with hair. The thing in the water, surging forward with tremendous power but with no apparent arm motion, was another of the same creatures. It was swimming towards the islet, which meant it was also swimming towards his boat. In panic, he got the motor going and sped off, but not before he got the impression that there might be two more of the creatures on the mainland beach."

Around this time, Titmus was on a sasquatch hunt by boat out of Klemtu. He learned about the sighting and was able to speak with both men. The second man didn't see the creatures, but told Titmus that he was on his way to meet his friend when the man

"tore by him at top speed headed back to Butedale and showed no sign of being aware that he was there."

A report from the Alaska Gold forum involves a trapper

working an area of the Ostuffna River near Lake Louise who saw several creatures he couldn't identify.

It was in June 1967 when the man had his first sighting. He observed what he first thought was a "lanky wolf" chasing some sheep in the area.

The following day, he got a better look and observed *"Three or four ape-like animals milling around the area like they were gathering for something."*

The man later spoke with a group of First Nations people who told him he'd seen *"Nackhanny."* The natives told him the creatures were *"…usually seen up Tsisi Creek behind Watna Mountain."*

Spring thaw

A report with scant details mentions an incident from August 1968. Reportedly a pair of hunters were driving along a mountain road when they spotted what they first thought was a bear. The men stopped their vehicle and got out to shoot at the animal. They received a shock when the animal walked off on two legs, moving up a hill and into the woods.

A report with more substance comes from a man working for a mining company in July 1969. The puzzling incident occurred in the Wrangell area.

In the summer of '69, the reporting witness, J.W. Huff was flown by helicopter to a camp in the Bradfield Canal area. Shortly after arriving, he spotted an unusual figure watching the camp. As he describes the incident:

"We were flown in by helicopter later in the afternoon and as soon as the 'copter was unloaded it immediately departed for Ketchikan. We started to get our camp up and prepare for the coming operations. While working on the camp shortly after the departure of the 'copter I happened to look up on a ridge about 300 feet (91.4m) *higher than we were and about 500 yards* (457m) *distant. I saw a man standing there watching us…"*

Naturally, Huff thought the figure was a normal person, perhaps another miner who had already staked a claim in the area. He thought that, if this were the case, he and his coworkers would have to pack up and depart, yielding to a previous claim. However, as he continued to look at the man on the ridge, he observed some very odd things.

"My partner and I watched this man for ten or fifteen minutes expecting him to come down to our camp and visit with us and inform us this was his area and, of course, we were prepared to tell him we would leave the next day. He stood absolutely motionless and we had a good look at him, and he appeared to be extremely large.

As we kept watching him, he seemed to have no hat of any kind and looked very dark and we had the impression he had no clothing on. After watching him, I resumed my work in getting the tent up while my partner continued to watch. He then yelled to this man and waved to him whereupon this man took off with a lumbering gait rather rapidly and soon disappeared over the ridge from our sight."

The miners continued to watch the area, expecting the man to come down from around the ridge and appear in their camp but he never showed up. Huff and his colleagues puzzled over the odd behavior. He later stated that if they had had their radio antenna up, he would have recalled the helicopter to sweep the area and see if the man could be spotted, unfortunately, all they could do was puzzle over the incident.

While the incident was fairly minor, it made an impression on Huff and must have nagged at the man and his coworkers. The next day, Huff and his colleague decided to investigate the ridge and see if they could find the odd man and solve the mystery.

"We had to decide where we were going to start our prospecting so we decided we might as well start where we had seen this huge man. It took us some time to get there as we had to take a roundabout route and were prospecting all the way. It was very warm and rainy, so the rocks were pretty slick, and we were taking our time. When we got to the place where this man had been standing, there were no tracks, of course, as it was bare rock. Nearby was a snowfield and we searched this area but could not find anything we could definitely pin down as tracks. There had been goats up on that same ridge the day before, but we could not find their tracks either due to the melting condition of the snow.

We did find some depressions in the snow that would require quite a bit of imagination to definitely call them tracks. This snowfield was rather small and once across it, bare rocks were once again encountered. What this thing was that we saw I do not know except that it was no known animal that I have ever encountered and all I can say is that I have never seen anything even approaching this thing. We were in that camp for about three weeks and never again saw a trace of him."

While Huff didn't have any further encounters with the big man, he did believe he'd had a sighting of one of the state's legendary Hairy Men. As he stated in the close of his report:

"I am writing this letter in answer to your request for information and have related these experiences to you just as I saw them and whether or not they are believed I personally could care less as I know

97

what I saw or at least what I appeared to see. I am fully positive that there is no reason that these sasquatch could not exist as there have been too many reported sightings of similar man-like creatures."

In 1970, Bob Betts collected numerous reports of sasquatch-like creatures in the Yukon River region. Betts was an anthropologist who worked for the Bureau of Land Management fire-fighting division for several summers while he was a student. He became intrigued by tales of what locals called the bushman in the summer of 1970 while traveling the region. Betts wrote to John Green about the stories:

"I've been getting out into the remote villages more than ever this year and have come up with some interesting information. The legend of the "Bushman" is widespread throughout interior Alaska. I've talked to natives from Huslia who claim people from their village have seen the "Bushman" recently, they describe it as larger than a man and completely covered with hair and very strong. I've also talked to natives from Allakaket and Tanana who also have a real belief in the "Bushman." The natives will not usually talk to outsiders about this."

Betts, along with a man named Jim McClarin and a team of researchers spent time researching around the village of Ruby. Local natives in the area told the team it was already too late in the year to see a bushman.

The bushmen, known in the local native tongue as *"Nakentlia"* were said to come into the area during the summer months. The nocturnal creatures were known to steal dried salmon from the village smokehouses, throw rocks and sticks at people and make a high-pitched whistle.

Despite the creature's reported absence, the team collected background information on the legend. They compiled 15 reports of encounters with the bushman. The incidents had taken place at towns and fish camps along the river. One sighting of note came from Paul Peters who said he saw a bushman on the beach near his fish camp ten miles (16km) west of the town of Ruby. The incident occurred in August 1960.

Peters said when the creature was about 75 yards (68.6m) away from him, it turned and climbed a steep hill and disappeared in the brush. The bipedal beast was tall and broad and covered with black hair.

Reportedly, members of the United States military had an encounter with a sasquatch in late 1970. The incident occurred at Black Rapids Glacier, south of the town of Delta Junction. The sighting was at long range, and one member of the unit reported on the incident:

"I was part of about a dozen Army personnel training in the area. I was looking across the valley when I spotted movement. It was moving up the valley about a half-mile (0.8km) away.

When it crossed the snow, you could plainly see that it was not a bear. It walked upright with long strides and arms swinging and moved fast. I have seen bears many times in the same type of terrain, and they do not move like this did. Bears can and do walk upright, usually for short distances when they need to see or smell something and need the height. They don't travel in this manner, and not in difficult terrain.

I pointed it out to the other guys, and we watched it until you could no longer see it. When it was out of the snow it was hard to see against the rocks. We wanted to go look at the tracks, but everyone was scared to go down there. We had to sleep there that night, and nobody would go outside after dark. The next day we got out and never went back.

Twenty years later, I still would not go up there even with a group and with guns.

It was dark in color. It was too big and fast to be human. The only thing I have seen that looked like this is descriptions of bigfoot."

Dolores Cline Brown, wife of Yukon Territory Hunting outfitter Louis Brown, spent a lot of time in the wilds of Alaska. She hunted and rode trails with her husband and recounted some of her adventures in a 1971 book, *"Yukon Trophy Trails."*

Brown writes of a night when she and a friend were roused by a loud knocking and banging against the door of their cabin. The pair didn't investigate and whatever it was went away, but another hunter told them he'd seen large, man-like tracks in the area early that day. He told Brown and her friend that it was a bushman and that if they saw it, they should *"kill him dead quick."*

In their book, *Artic Homestead: The True Story of One Family's Survival and Courage in the Alaskan Wilds,* authors Norma Cobb and Charles W. Sasser relate a strange story of the hairy man they heard during their adventures.

Cobb and her family moved to the wilds of Alaska in 1973 and during their adventures, heard a number of curious tales. One of note came from an elderly woman Cobb refers to as a "medicine woman." The title was due to the woman's experiences as a young girl in Alaska's interior. It seems the woman was captured by a hairy giant. As the authors relate:

"She was out picking berries with others near Rampart when she was kidnapped by a Bushman. She was taken into the wilderness and brought to a cave, where she saw other members of the Hairy Man's family or group.

In that cave, there were both male and female Hairy Man people, and even younger ones. They were hairy and wore no clothes and smelled badly. But one of the babies of the Hairy Man people was very sick."

The tale treads further into supernatural territory as it's revealed that the hairy creatures "spoke to her without talking." In what was apparently some form of mental communication, the woman learned she had been brought to the cave so she could help heal the sick child.

The woman did her best to aid the hairy infant and after an unspecified time, the baby made a recovery. Once the child was healed, the hairy people let the woman go, but not before specifying that she should tell no one where they lived. The woman agreed and a bushman took the woman back to her village.

Reportedly, the bushmen told the woman that they were afraid of showing themselves to humans because they didn't want to be chased or shot at.

With its more fantastical aspects, the story may be uncomfortable for researchers who believe the creatures are nothing more than an undiscovered animal species, but the tale does reflect aspects of Native Alaskan spiritual concepts wherein the bushman is considered another race of intelligent beings.

One account reported by Robert Alley that's especially noteworthy is the one from Mr. Harold A., a Sitka commercial fisherman. The incident occurred in the summer of 1979, although it was not reported until 1999. The witness was working on the west coast of Baranof Island, about 32 miles (51km) south of Sitka. Has he reports:

"We had our fifty-two-foot (15.8m) seiner, then getting some use as a fish packer, up at the south end of Cedar Pass, and it was late. We were just finishing anchoring up for the night about 100 yards (91.4m) from shore and we were settled. My crew was below tending to securing gear. I was alone in the cabin, resting at the galley table with the starboard porthole window open above my elbow, with the cabin light on as usual. It was dark outside.

Just then, I felt something lift my right arm and looked up to see a huge hairy arm. Its arm was covered with dark brown fur and I could see the whole forearm up to near the elbow. The hand was palm up and huge, being about three times the size of a human hand. The skin was a dirty brownish gray color. The whole of the arm except the palm side of the hand was covered with four-inch (10cm) dark brown or black hair. I could not tell if there was a thumb. I wasn't being squeezed or anything, just lifted up, and I would have to say it felt gentle. But I can tell you, I hollered and pulled my arm away, and I didn't even look outside! I got the engine started and the crew to pull anchor and we moved north up the channel about five or six miles (8 – 10km) to a new spot before deciding that would be a better spot to anchor for the night. We didn't hear or see anything else that time."

1980s-1990s

The *Delta Discovery* received testimony from a man who said he encountered a hairy creature while dog mushing in the 1980s.

The incident happened in late December or early January, though the witness wasn't sure of the year. He was a young man between the ages of ten and 12 when he saw the creature. At the time, he was in the Petersville area leading a six-dog sled team. He recalls that he had just passed the Kenny Creek "valley" and was going slowly uphill. It was around 10:30 at night and there was bright moonlight.

"Everything was dead quiet too; even the dogs were panting lightly, going up that hill that night. I was halfway up the hill at the time when I happened to look behind me and saw something walking from one side of the road. It had just walked from the creek in the valley.

I kept looking at what I saw while I was moving up. The being stopped halfway in the middle of the road and I saw it looking at me. This was no bear; it was tall and walked upright—like a human.

I froze at the sight of the creature; I didn't say or do anything as the dogs crept forward and I could do nothing but look back at it.

This being stared at me. It did not do anything either, other than keep staring at me. Then, as I inched away, the being moved and walked to the other side of the road.

There is no chance this was a bear. This was not a human being either. There are no houses in the area."

Even to this day, the man has no explanation for what he saw while mushing that cold night.

Aleut elder Ted Angasan had a sighting of the Hairy Man in 1985. Angasan was on a commercial flight traveling from Kululak Bay to Dillingham. While passing over forested mountains near the village of Manokotak, Angasan saw an unusual creature:

"There was this giant thing sitting in the trees. He looked like, not quite a gorilla, but dark and full of hair. I'd say, from the trees around him, he was between seven and ten feet (2.1 – 3m) tall."

Majestic Denali rises over the Alaskan landscape

In 1992, a couple driving between Anchorage and Fairbanks saw a creature near Denali Park. The couple was in a 1980 Dodge D50, a truck sitting low to the ground. It was nighttime when the pair spotted the thing in the vehicle's headlights. As the witness reported:

"It was late at night, and we were just about to the tourist Area of the Denali Park. It wasn't winter yet, just before a corner, my lights hit something sitting on the yellow line in the middle of the road. The lights to this truck were grossly out of adjustment, so they were pointing right at the thing. It was sitting in the middle of the road with its legs pulled up to its chest, and its arms folded over its knees. Its head was between its arms, looking toward the ground. It had long, human like hair...at first, I thought it was an orangutan. Then I thought to myself, what would an orangutan be doing in the middle of nowhere in Alaska?"

The witness stated he had lived in the state for most of his life and knew there was no known animal in the state that fit the appearance of what he was seeing.

"I thought to myself the only way that could have been an orangutan is if there's a circus out here...I knew that was not a possibility in such a remote area. I drove right next to it and I was at its level. If I had been going slow, I could have touched it easily. I was freaked out and thought I must be seeing things, maybe I was tired."

As it turned out, the truck's passenger also spotted the creature, though nothing was discussed until the pair reached a gas station in the town of Healy. Both witnesses were shaken up by the sighting:

"This spooked us so bad we didn't even say anything to each other about it until we were around people. We have talked about this, and still agree that we saw this thing. We have given up on trying to explain it to anyone else, because no one believes it anyway."

A man hunting around Goldstream Valley in the Fairbanks area had a strange experience in August 1997.

The weather was clear and beautiful the day the veteran outdoorsman set out for a hunting trip in the valley. After a full day of hunting, including a close run-in with a bear, the man chose a spot and settled in for the evening. He was sleeping out in the open under a spruce tree, with no tent. A while after he'd tucked in, something came into his camp:

"Sometime in the middle of the night, I was awakened by something prowling around my camp, maybe thirty feet (9.1m) or so away from me, walking in a circle...this was not a bear I heard in the night. My father is a hunting guide, and I literally grew up hunting bears. I KNOW what a bear sounds like when it's walking. Whatever this thing was, it was walking on two legs, with a bit of a shuffling sound between each step, like it was dragging its feet a bit. The leaves on the forest floor were dry like potato chips, and it was breaking a lot of branches—I could hear it and follow its movements quite distinctly."

Having spent so much of his time in the wilds of Alaska, the man was familiar with all the state's creatures, at least, he thought he was. But whatever was in his camp that night greatly disturbed him. As he continues:

"I have to say that I've spent a LOT of time in the Alaskan bush and have never before or since been truly afraid of anything I've encountered, but I don't mind saying that on that particular night I was literally shaking with fear.

It circled my camp for what seemed like hours, but it was probably only five minutes or so. Finally, remembering something I had once read about the Athabascan Indians' beliefs regarding "woodsmen," I started talking to it, albeit in a shaky voice, saying I wanted no trouble that night. The thing stopped dead in its tracks, then a few moments later, I heard it trotting downhill, away from me. Talking to such a creature may sound kinda cornball, but all I know is that it worked."

The next morning, the man packed his gear and resumed his hunting, working his way back home. He notes *"I've kicked myself for this many times since but the next morning, I didn't bother to look for any tracks, hair, etc."*

He did tell investigators that he recalled hearing a *"low muttering sound"* as the creature was moving around his camp site. He had no further problems with the unseen creature and continues to hunt in the area.

A BFRO report details a May 22, 1998 sighting that took place near Fort Wainwright in Fairbanks County. The man who posted the report states clearly that he didn't see the creature himself, though a noncommissioned officer he worked with did. The officer, his wife and child, and a hunting buddy were in a vehicle on their way home at the time of the incident. The man reports:

"...according to them a large, hairy about seven-foot (2.1m) *ape looking thing crossed the road in front of them. From what I could gather none of them are too familiar with bigfoot information. Anyway, they say it crossed the road which is about thirty-five feet* (10.7m) *in width in four to five steps it seemed, and disappeared into the brush on the other side which leads to a river called the Chena.*

Both of the guys have been hunting since childhood and are sure they know a bear when they see one. The thing crossed the road on its hind legs and as we all agreed, yeah, a bear can raise up on its hindlegs and even take a few clumsy steps, but, cross a thirty-five-foot (10.7m) *road...naw!"*

The men later returned to the scene and looked for the thing's tracks. They found prints unlike any they had encountered in all their years of hunting. The tracks were "pointed inward" as if the maker was "pigeon-toed." Nothing else was found at the scene at the time.

The man reporting the sighting was clear the incident took place on the grounds of the military installation. Notes on the case file indicate the location of the incident was a road called Trainor Gate, a rural section that leads to Birch Hill, an area where a lot of military personnel went to ski.

The two men who witnessed the creature were not interested in coming forward as they feared ridicule.

The region around the base is rugged wilderness. Woods, rocks and hills cover the area and there is abundant wildlife and vegetation. The Chena River is also nearby so there is ample fresh water.

Hydaburg in Prince of Wales County has been the location of a number of sasquatch sightings over the years. Hydaburg is a small town on the north shore of Sukkwan Strait. It's the southernmost city on the island and has a small population of just under 400 residents.

First Nations people in the area say a hairy creature they call the *Guugiit* has long lived in the region.

There was a string of sightings in the area in the late 1990s. One witness driving on Saltery Road saw a creature between a sort-yard and garbage dump in the Spring of 1995. As reported to the BFRO:

"I had three kids with me, my daughters and one of their cousins. It was starting to get dark. I decided I wanted to turn around and not go all the way down to the sort yard. So, I pulled into a turnaround. I had the car lights on. Just in the bushes on the other side of the road, I noticed some movement.

I thought it might have been a deer, so I stopped the car. The first thing I really saw was really bright blue eyes. Then I noticed how far up they were, the thing had to be about 8-9 feet (2.4 – 2.7m) tall. The rest of the thing was real dark, might have been black or dark brown. My daughter saw the feet…they were huge.

When I realized it might be a bigfoot, I freaked out and tore out of there. I've never been down there after dark again. I rarely go there at all. It didn't move after the initial movement we saw, it just stood there looking at us."

The creature may have been in the area scrounging in the garbage for food scraps. Other people in the area reported seeing the thing rooting in trash piles and garbage cans.

One witness reported seeing the creature bent over digging in garbage in the Spring of 1996. When the beast realized someone had spotted it, it stood up and quickly left the area, ducking away and out of sight in several quick strides.

The Hairy Man was estimated to be between eight and nine feet (2.4 – 2.7m) tall with dark hair covering its body.

A woman I spoke with told me that in 1999, she was visiting the area and spotted a tall, hairy creature ripping open a trash bag. It was early evening and she was driving alone. The creature didn't seem to notice her at first and she thought it may have been preoccupied with whatever was in the bag. When it realized there was a car approaching, it quickly ran off into the woods taking the bag of trash with it.

As with previous cases, the bigfoot was reported as being dark colored and at least seven feet (2.1m) tall.

2000s

Sightings from the same region continued into the 2000s. In February 2004, a woman reported one of the hairy bipeds prowling around her home just outside of Hydaburg.

"My daughter was home alone. She lives with a relative, who was out of town. She called me at 11:22 pm; she was terrified. She said she could hear something walking back and forth by her bedroom window. She also said she looked out the window when she first heard it and saw 'something' big and black, really big. She described the 'thing' to have been about 3-4 feet (0.9 – 1.2m) above the bottom of the window.

When I went down to look behind the house this morning, I stood by the window. I am 5'4" (1.65m) and my eyes just reach the bottom of the window, so I figure this 'thing' must have been 7-8 feet (2.1 – 2.4m) tall."

The Alaska-Canadian Highway (ALCAN) is known as a scenic route with ample opportunity to catch glimpses of Alaska's varied wildlife. The region is rich in forest, mountains and thousands of lakes. But a man and his daughter traveling the highway in the summer of 2004 spotted something not found in state wildlife guides.

It was Friday, June 18th, and the pair were traveling westbound, about 30-45 minutes from the US Customs Office at the Alaska/Canadian border. They were hauling a 27ft. (8.2m) trailer and enjoying the drive and the view as they talked and listened to music. The driver hit the brakes when he saw an odd creature on the side of the road. The man describes the sighting:

"An object caught my eye standing in the tree line south of the eastbound lane. I saw something from the waist up reaching to a higher part of a white bark tree. I did a double take and slammed on the brakes and came to a complete stop. Whatever it was had its back to us and still was reaching up with its right arm. The animal was a beautiful blonde/auburn coloration and appeared well groomed, as I could see the waist and well-developed shoulder that blended into the head. I didn't see a real neck. I made a mental note using the tree as a

height-measuring device."

The man alerted his daughter and grabbed his camera, but by the time he was out of the truck, the creature had vanished. He surveyed the location where the bigfoot had been standing. Using the mental note he had made, he was able to estimate that the creature was at least nine feet (2.7m) in height with an overhead reach better than twelve feet (3.7m).

A few years later, another pair of travelers on the ALCAN Highway had a bigfoot sighting.

It was April 23, 2008. The reporting witness was riding in the passenger seat of a vehicle being driven by his son. They were traveling on the highway near Tok at around 6:45 in the evening. The location of the sighting is close to the Canadian border, approximately fifteen miles (24km) from the US Customs Office.

The man was watching the scenery, hoping to see some of the area's wildlife when he spotted something much more unusual than a bear or moose. As he reports:

"…I saw what I thought was a human crossing the road, maybe 3-tenths of a mile (0.4km) ahead of us and up the slight incline. He was a tall, odd looking fellow and I joked to myself when I first saw him…'Well, there is a sasquatch up the road' fully expecting to see that a person had crossed from a house or something on the left-hand side of the road over to another house or something on the right-hand side."

As the car approached the area however, the man quickly realized there were no houses or buildings around. Nothing for a human to have come out of. A closer look at the figure confirmed that it wasn't a human at all. The creature was between eight and nine feet (2.4 – 2.7m) tall and there was no distinction between its head and neck.

"This thing was walking upright like a man, long arms and what looked like a long neck from the side. It had a fairly long gap in his walk…arms swinging with each stride. It was all one color…I described it to my wife as the color of a Carhartt rust/brown full coveralls."

A man driving on Yoder road, 16 miles (26km) from Talkeetna, saw a sasquatch in July 2008.

The witness said the dark-colored creature was on a flat section of road when he spotted it. At first, the man thought he was seeing the largest black bear he'd ever seen, but within moments he realized he wasn't looking at a bear at all. He estimated the bipedal creature was between seven and a half to eight feet (2.3 – 2.4m) in height. It was covered with jet black hair around six inches (15cm) in length.

According to the witness, the hairy creature turned its upper body to look at him. It had a *"fleshy face, no hair on cheeks and forehead."* The creature didn't hang around the area very long once it realized it was being observed:

"It walked into the woods after spotting me. I then raced the car up to that spot and slowly drove by looking into the foliage. You couldn't see into the woods, too much foliage. It looked…extremely well-muscled…looked tremendously strong! There was no V shape of the back, the back was straight to the waist where the "lat" muscles would be on a man."

When I was in Alaska in 2018, a witness told me he'd witnessed a Hairy Man ten years previously (2008) just outside of Talkeetna.

The streets of Talkeetna

"It was tall, between six and seven feet (1.8 – 2.1m) tall, hairy and black. It was moving across an open area away from the road. It was headed for the trees and moving with long strides. I stopped to get a good look at it and as I was standing there, it turned and looked at me. It slowed way down when it was looking at me, honestly it was unnerving. But it kept going and, in a moment, resumed the faster pace. Once it hit the tree line, it was out of sight pretty quick. I stood there for a few minutes just amazed. I knew what it was. I started to leave, then had a second thought and went over to look at the tracks. The track line was clear in the snow, but the snow was coming down enough that the tracks were already getting obscured."

A daytime sighting of a reddish-colored bigfoot occurred near Fairbanks in the Summer of 2009.

It was July when the witness was traveling south on Auburn Drive towards Farmers Loop. The witness was on the section of road that passes by Pearl Creek Elementary School. The school can be seen through the woods, though the trees are thick in some areas around it.

According to the report, some areas around the school had been heavily cleared, giving a good sightline towards the school and a vegetable garden on the property.

At six o'clock in the evening, the witness was heading home after a day of work. The weather was clear and the sun high in the sky.

"As I was driving, I happened to notice a 'man' standing by the right side of the road about 100 yards (91m) ahead. It was more of an unconscious recognition. There's nothing unusual about a man standing on the side of the road in this area. As I got to within about 50 yards (47m), I looked closer. 'That's no man' I said to myself (I was alone in the car).

Shortly after that, one or two seconds, he bolted into the woods towards the school. He did it like a wild animal would do if spooked."

The driver stopped at the spot where he'd seen the figure enter the woods. He could still see it running away from the road about 30 yards (27m) away. The figure then turned and started running parallel to the road, giving the witness a better view.

"I got a good look at him, but not his face. I could have probably seen his face had I not been so mesmerized and had the presence of mind to look at it. I was busy noticing other things.

His fur or hair looked to be about three to four inches (8 – 10cm) all over the main part of his body. It was a reddish rusty color.

I was mildly struck by how red it was, but it definitely had some rustiness to it. He was about six feet (1.8m) tall and looked to weigh about 200 lbs (91kg). He ran with a strange "Hoppy" kind of run. It wasn't a limp. With one foot he pushed off with what was more a normal running move, but the other foot he pushed off with propelled him upward (about a foot (0.3m) or less) and forward."

The witness watched the bigfoot until it had completely vanished into the trees. A check of the area revealed no further glimpses of the creature.

The following day, the driver stopped in the area to see if by any chance the creature had returned. He spotted a couple walking their dogs and stopped them to talk, relating the previous day's encounter to them.

"...they told me that about a week before they were with their dogs and were on the way to the other side of the school property by the soccer field, and three kids came running over to them saying 'Did you see the sasquatch, did you see the sasquatch?'"

In a follow up interview with a BFRO investigator, the witness reaffirmed that he didn't get a clear look at the creature's face. However, he described the thing's head as being *"a cross between that of a human and a gorilla."* The hair was described as being fairly uniform in length and estimated at three to four inches (8 – 10cm) in length.

In the winter of 2011, a man riding a snowmobile between Hooper Bay and Scammon encountered a Hairy Man and got within 20 feet (6m) of it. The witness was on the Paimuit Trail, heading towards Hooper Bay. The trip is approximately 30 miles (48km), and the man had made the same journey on many occasions.

At the time of the sighting, the man was on the Hooper Bay side of the hills going up a hill that led to a lake. He spotted a figure on the trail ahead of him and at first thought it was a person wearing a big, thick parka. He drove towards the figure, thinking perhaps someone had broken down on the trail and they were walking to Hooper Bay.

The closer he got to the figure, the more he realized it was something unusual.

"Its arms were really long, and it seemed to be hairy all over. Its hair was like a musk-ox, but brown."

The man felt very uneasy, so when he was around 60 - 70 feet (18 – 21m) away from the figure, he turned his machine to the right of him instead of continuing on a path straight to him.

Even more puzzling, the figure was ignoring the sound of the snowmobile and didn't even turn to look at the witness. When the witness got to within 20 feet (6m) of the walker, the figure finally turned towards him. The witness was shocked to see red eyes staring at him:

"I think I screamed and hollered at that moment, but I don't know."

He realized the figure in front of him was not human, the next thing he recalls, he was gunning his machine and taking off as quickly as possible. In his haste, the man hit a bump that caused the machine to jump and land in the lake. He almost lost control but regained it, and continued at high speed until he reached Hooper Bay.

He went immediately to his parent's house and told them what he had encountered.

The man was so shaken, that when he returned to Scammon Bay, he took the long route and had one of his brothers join him for the trip.

"I didn't want to run into that thing again."

Two teenage boys and their mother spotted a bigfoot near the village of Kasigluk in the spring of 2012. The trio were on the outskirts of the village riding a 4-wheeler when they spotted the creature. It was large, dark and hairy.

The family recalls that the incident took place on May 29th, at about three o'clock in the afternoon. The weather was beautiful, and they were enjoying the day.

"We came across it by the lagoon here in Kasigluk, it was back there southeast of Fox Lake. After it passed, we looked at each other and thought, 'we just saw Bigfoot.'"

The creature was about 75 yards (69m) away. It was described as very tall and dark, with long arms that hung below its knees. The witnesses estimate they watched the creature for about two minutes.

"It was walking towards us and then once it saw us, it turned and started going to the other side of the hill."

The bigfoot quickly vanished into the bushes. The mother wrote out her full account of the sighting, it reads in part:

"Upon reaching the lagoon my older son got off the four-wheeler

and ran off to see if anybody was in that area. He ran to the edge of the hill and soon ran back saying that somebody was already there. So, we decided to go check somewhere else when that 'somebody' started running at an incredible speed. No human person would have gone from down there by that flat land to already towards us up the hill.

That 'somebody' was all black from top to bottom, kind of hunchbacked, like it had no neck and its head was cone shaped. Its long arms went past its knees and it was incredibly tall.

At first, we all asked each other, 'Who is that?' Then after about ten seconds as it was walking with long strides it would occasionally look towards us. The way it walked was fast and no human could cover that amount of tundra in the same amount of time."

As the sighting quickly ended, the witnesses realized they'd seen a bigfoot:

"We went up to the top of the hill, but we didn't see it anywhere, so we went straight home feeling kind of excited."

A worker at the Napakiak Village Corporation spotted a bigfoot in late April 2013. The witness was on the second floor of the building, looking out of the window when she saw the creature. It was walking on top of a bluff on the other side of the Napakiak Slough.

The creature was dark colored and walking on two feet. The witness stated that she had seen people on the bluff in the past and was certain it wasn't a human:

"It was real unusual, too tall to be a person. It was taller than the brush on top of the bluff."

As the witness watched, the creature walked down to the lower part of the bluff and vanished, but it soon reappeared. The woman dashed downstairs and got the attention of several people below, asking them to come up and see the creature.

Eight people joined the witness upstairs and they all observed the hairy beast.

At the time of the sighting, the ground still had some snow on it. The witnesses noticed a group of children sledding down the bluff. The children noticed the beast and ran away in terror.

As the witnesses continued to watch the creature on the bluff, a snowmobiler came up over the hill. Although the driver of the snowmobile didn't see the bigfoot, the creature reacted to the sound of the machine. It hid by ducking down on the ground so that it was out of view of the driver.

After the snowmobile had passed, the creature went over the hill and disappeared in a northwesterly direction.

The witness noted that the day before the sighting, a lone ice fisherman near Napakiak had reportedly seen a group of the creatures in the area.

A man out four-wheeling had a strange sighting around Hooper Bay. Bosco Wilson was looking for driftwood on July 4, 2014 when he spotted the creature. It was just after eight a.m. when he saw something black feeding on a walrus carcass. According to Wilson, the carcass had been rotting for at least five days.

At first glance, and from a distance, Wilson thought he was seeing a large raven on the carcass. In moments, he realized the figure was much larger, and in fact, it was larger than a normal person.

Bosco says he and the creature looked at each other for a time. As he observed, the creature walked around, picked up a heavy piece of driftwood and went back to the carcass. The creature tried to use the driftwood as a lever to turn over the dead walrus. It soon became frustrated and walked away from the area altogether.

Bosco returned to the site the next day and investigated the carcass. He found a steak knife buried in the decaying carcass.

The creature was estimated to be around nine feet (2.7m) tall.

In September 2016, *Anchorage Daily News* reporter Ben Anderson wrote an article on bigfoot sightings in northern Alaska. Highlighting reports from a Barrow area family, Anderson posed the question:

"Is there a Bigfoot on Alaska's North Slope? One Barrow family thinks so, and it has them worried about a remote cabin property

they own about 35 miles (56km) *south of America's northernmost community."*

The story detailed accounts from a woman named Sarah Skin who had been using the cabin for years. The cabin itself lies between Barrow and the community of Atqasku. Over the three previous years, Skin and her family had been encountering creatures in the region. According to her, the beasts were massive:

"...10-foot (3m) *tall, bipedal creatures that are black, brown or grayish in color."*

Skin called the creature a bigfoot and said that prior to the sightings near her family cabin, she had never seen anything like it.

"People from a long time ago used to see them, I guess. I'm 50 years old and I've been camping out here my whole life, and I've never seen anything like this, ever."

Skin reported a September sighting by her sons Joe and Edgar who were hunting caribou when they saw a bigfoot. They estimated that it was ten feet (3m) tall. According to Skin:

"They saw one about a mile (1.6km) *from my cabin, there was big herd of caribou coming toward them and suddenly this big black creature started chasing them."*

Skin also reported damages to the family cabin, as well as a sturdy meat rack that was torn down.

Some people think Skin's problem isn't sasquatch, but bears. The area certainly has a population of bears and the animals could be the culprits in some of the incidents, however, to simply write the case off in such a manner means either the family is lying, or completely mistaken in what they've witnessed. Since the family has long associations with the region, it's difficult to believe they are unfamiliar with bear sightings and behavior. Besides, the family has reported seeing the creatures "running on two legs," something that bears don't do.

The woman reached out to various sources for help, but no one responded to her. Unfortunately, she has no evidence to show beyond personal accounts and sightings. She's not deterred though:

"Nobody's volunteered to help us, so it's going to be a family effort to try to get some photographs."

On January 23, 2018, a 7.9 magnitude earthquake struck the Gulf of Alaska near Kodiak Island. The quake was felt throughout southern Alaska including the cities of Anchorage and Fairbanks, as well as parts of neighboring British Columbia.

A tsunami warning was issued for the region and officials were on high alert. Residents of low-lying areas along the Gulf of Alaska and in British Columbia were evacuated and sent to safety shelters.

Fortunately for people in the region, no tsunami ever manifested, and the danger passed. But in the aftermath of the earthquake and tsunami threat, a series of reports surfaced from the village of Sitka.

Writer and veteran cryptozoologist Loren Coleman reported on his blog Cryptozoonews, that he was contacted by an Alaskan cryptid investigator who had details of some of the accounts. Reportedly, three native families saw *"Bigfoot-like creatures heading up the hills to higher grounds."* Multiple tracks were also found in the area.

The reporting investigator, being a Tlingit, was able to communicate with locals without cultural barriers. As a result, he learned more than an outside investigator would be able to in a short period of time.

Coleman received details on several incidents. For privacy purposes, names of witnesses were changed in the reports. The first incident occurred just as cell phones in the area were receiving alerts for the tsunami warning. Residents of Sitka were gathering personal items so they could evacuate. The investigator told Coleman about an encounter reported to him by a man he calls Eric:

"Bears which would normally be hibernating, were heading to higher ground as well along with deer. Eric was out at Starrgavin park, a popular place for people locally which is several miles away

from downtown Sitka.

The alert came over Eric's cell phone. Eric and his girlfriend started back towards town in their car. Having just passed the Alaska Marine highway ferry system terminal, they were going around a bend in the road. Eric's car died on the spot. They sat for a few moments trying to restart the car. Eric popped the hood to see what was going on with his car. He got out of the car.

A deer was running across the road. A moment later a humanoid figure standing approximately eight feet (2.4m) tall crossed the road directly in front of them. The creature was just a few feet away from their car."

The investigator questioned the man closely. The witness was positive the creature wasn't a known animal, in fact, he believed it was a creature from native legend:

"That was no bear. I know it definitely wasn't human. That was a Kooshtakaa...He paused briefly in front of our car. He looked right at us. I was more fascinated than I was scared at the moment. You could see his hair-covered body."

The witness continued describing details of the creature's appearance:

"His arms seemed a little disproportionate compared to a human. They seemed longer. It just looks different from our arms. His biceps/triceps were definitely bigger than any human I've ever seen...I stood there by my car door. He paused and looked at me straight in the eyes. He looked like he was about ready to come towards me but then he took off continuing across the road and into the woods. My God, that smell about him was awful. I've never smelled anything like that."

Another incident reported to Coleman by the same investigator involves the Johns family. The family's home was at high enough elevation that they didn't need to evacuate during the tsunami warning. While monitoring conditions, they lost power at their home. The children were asleep, and their mother was looking for candles when the father, Michael, stepped outside. As the report reads:

"There he was. He was so huge! He started coming towards the house. I fell backwards on my butt. I yelled at him to get away. I didn't

119

know what else to do.

He was right by the shed. I don't think he could come in the door without ducking down."

Measurements indicated the creature was between eight and eight and a half feet (2.4 – 2.6m) tall.

A third incident in the area could not be documented in detail.

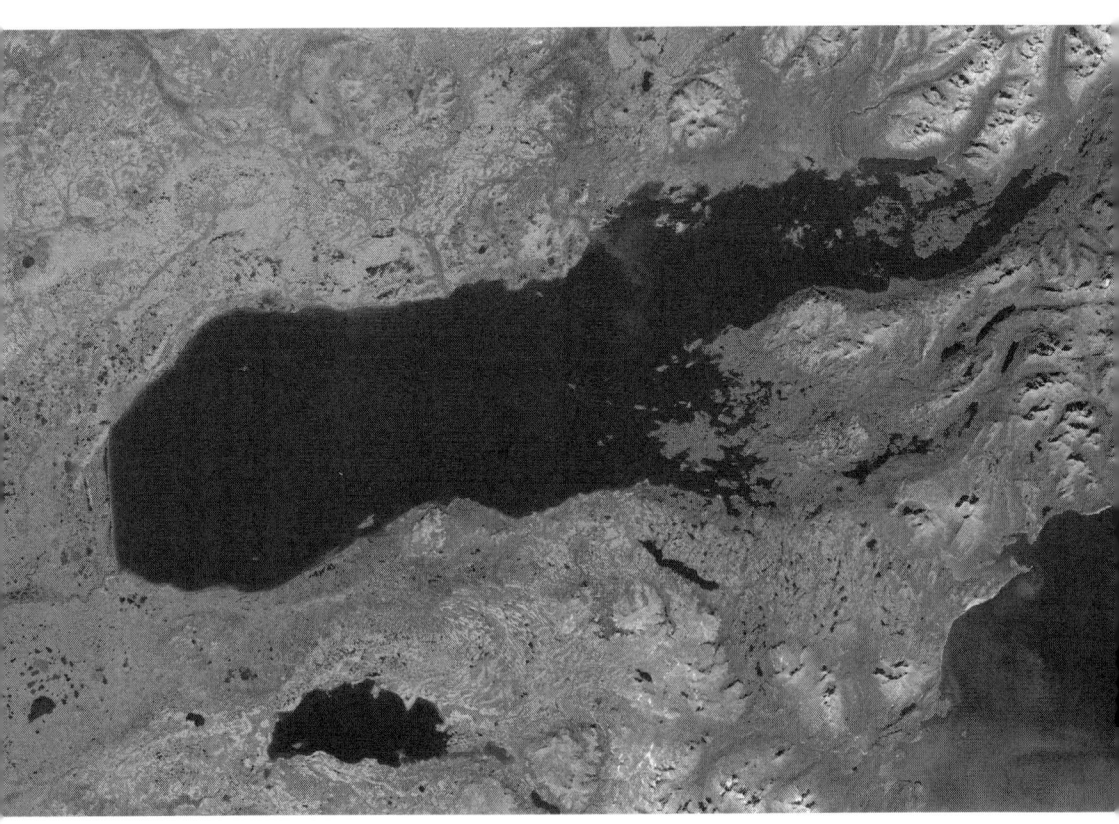

Satellite image shows Iliamna Lake and surrounding area.

The Lake Iliamna Hairy Man

Lake Iliamna is no stranger to monster tales. While its well-known as the domain of a monster lurking in the depths of its cold waters, there's also another creature spoken of in the area—the "big man."

For years, tales of the hairy giant have been a part of local legend among the lake's communities. First Nations people in the region say the creature, one that's described as a typical bigfoot, has lived in the forest surrounding Lake Iliamna for decades.

The creature is known to wander the vast wilderness around the lake, and at times, it comes near villages in the area.

Inevitably, stories of the area's bigfoot started getting out to the media.

Gerken's Gamble

In 1977, retired U.S. Coast Guard Commander Ted Gerken decided to pursue a dream. He and his wife Mary took on ownership of a wilderness lodge on Lake Iliamna in western Alaska. It was a challenge, but one the couple was up for as they undertook a different phase of their lives. Gerken chronicled many of his adventures running the lodge in a book, published in 1988, titled "*Gamble at Iliamna.*"

Gerken writes about the various oddball characters he encountered, as well as the challenges he and his wife faced running a business in the rugged territory. In the midst of his fascinating accounts, there's the tale of an encounter with the "big man."

Gerken writes about Jim Coffee, a friend he made in Alaska. Coffee was a maintenance man assigned to the Iliamna

Flight Service Station. Gerken describes Coffee as a man *"in his mid-fifties, of average height and build, with graying hair and a ruddy complexion."*

Coffee had a strange encounter one January when he was driving his pickup truck to the airport during a light snow. Less than half a mile from his home, his headlights caught the outline of a large animal. Coffee said the creature was "potbellied, covered with dark hair, and about nine feet (2.7m) tall."

Apparently, the beast was startled by the vehicle. It was running upright on two legs and moved off the road quickly, heading into the brush beside the road.

Coffee pulled out a pistol, a powerful .357 Magnum, and took several shots at the thing.

The man never explained what led him to shoot at the bipedal creature. Maybe it was a typical Alaskan frontier style reaction, or maybe he was just as shocked by the sighting as the creature was.

Gerken doubted the sighting was genuine. He knew Coffee was fond of taking a drink or two on occasion and thought it could explain the account. Still, he was curious enough to pursue the tale. The day after the sighting, Gerken and his wife drove out to the spot where Coffee had seen the creature. As he recounts:

"I admit to being somewhat skeptical about the whole thing—but there was no harm looking. A light powdery snow had been falling at the time, so whatever he saw, it should have left tracks.

And, indeed, something had. A trail of large footprints in the fresh snow led along the edge of the road, so we got out to take a closer look. Each footprint measured 22" (56cm) from toe to heel, with a width across the three toes of 12" (30cm) and across the heel of 36"(91cm) and the track led straight down the edge of the road."

Gerken started to think the entire thing was a hoax, assuming someone had made replicas of giant feet using snowshoes. His opinion changed however, when he realized the tracks not only crossed the road, but continued into difficult terrain:

"I could clearly see each footprint dug into the side of the snow berm, with the uphill side of the track definitely cut deeper into the hill than the downhill side. I didn't believe a man with plywood snowshoes could make such tracks on a hill. And they definitely weren't the tracks of either a brown bear or a moose, the largest animals known in this area."

In short order, talk of the creature, or, "big man," spread around the nearby villages of Iliamna and Newhalen. The creature wasn't a new topic for native people in the region. Older accounts from Newhalen stated that whole families of bigfoot had previously lived in the area and frequently ventured close to the village. Children were warned to leave them alone and stay out of their paths so that no harm would befall the community.

Across the lake, residents of another village, Kakhonak, reported early encounters with the big man. One tale involved an incident when one of the creatures was caught in a net. The villagers locked the beast in a shed in hopes of containing it, but during the night, it escaped.

Living at Lake Iliamna and hearing about the big man firsthand, Gerken became intrigued by the tales. He says one of the most convincing accounts came from Connie Wassillie, a cook hired to work at the lodge during the busy summer months.

Connie was a white woman who had married a local native man. They lived in a cabin near the Roadhouse airstrip less than half a mile (.08km) (through the woods) from the road where Jim Coffee had spotted the creature.

Around the time Coffee had his sighting, Wassillie was visiting a neighbor. After her visit, she and her son James, a toddler, headed back to her own cabin. The following day, she told Mary Gerken her story.

While walking across the yard to her cabin, Wassillie had the unsettling feeling that she was being watched. Once in her house, she locked the door behind her and got on with her daily chores. After bathing her young son, she opened the door to throw out the tub of bath water. When she opened the door, she was hit by a powerful animal odor that she described as *"rotten and nauseating."* She quickly closed and relocked the doors.

The following morning, she found the outside door open and two pies she'd left out to cool missing. Just off the steps, she discovered the biggest footprints she'd ever seen. The footprints went around the cabin and to her bedroom window. From there, the tracks went towards a neighbor's house.

Myrtle, the neighbor, reported sheets and pillowcases stolen from her clothesline. There was speculation that the creature had been hit by one of Jim Coffee's bullets and used the sheets to bandage itself, though no one reported finding a trail of blood.

After the incidents, Gerken met Jim Repine, an authority on fishing in Alaska, and an Anchorage television personality. He told Repine about the recent sightings and the man was fascinated.

"I'd love to do a piece on it for the paper," Repine told him.

Gerken tried to set up some interviews for the story, but once a hint of the media was mentioned, native people in the area clammed up. By the time Repine showed up to do his report, only a couple of people (non-natives) were willing to talk to him.

Gerken says locals became almost protective of the big man and just didn't want large scale attention focused on the creature:

"Myth or fact, it remains a mystery to us—but the natives know that there's something out there in the dark, watching."

Repine wasn't deterred by the lack of cooperation. He understood local reluctance to discuss the hairy man:

"They fear that, once again, outsiders will find reasons to ridicule them as being backward and superstitious. They don't like all this publicity because it does attract strangers to the villages. Most important and seldom pointed out, they have a protective feeling toward a creature with whom they have lived peacefully for centuries."

Repine and his cameraman filmed a trackway that the seasoned outdoorsman found quite impressive. As he reported:

"As for the footprints we filmed...I've been more than a casual observer of animal tracks for over thirty years. I believe those were made by a creature walking upright, whose weight far exceeded that of a human being."

Even without local cooperation, Alaskan news sources ran stories on the big man sightings. In January 1978, the *Anchorage News* ran several features on the creature. The concerns voiced by locals seemed to be validated since hunters reportedly descended on the area, guns in hand, hoping to bag the mysterious beast.

The would-be monster hunters apparently had no luck finding the creature and eventually lost interest.

Bill Wilson, sports editor for the *Anchorage Daily News*, interviewed those involved in the sightings, at least, those who would talk to him. Wilson quickly learned the same lesson others had; local natives didn't want to discuss the big man.

One elderly woman did respond when Wilson asked her what she would do if she saw one of the big men. She responded:

"I'd be scared, but I wouldn't shoot. These creatures travel in pairs, sometimes two and three. You see, they have families, just like us. They're not too smart like people, but they know what is going on. They eat fish. I know they steal a lot from the villages. I guess they might eat berries too. But they do not eat meat."

The woman told Wilson that the creatures had been in the area for a long, long time, noting:

"When the old people here were young, the Big Men used to come by and poke sticks at them and throw rocks."

Bill Wilson himself finds stories of the big man compelling and believes there's something unexplained out there.

"Until you prove to me that there is no Big Man, I'm not writing off anything I saw. I saw a bunch of footprints. B-i-g footprints."

There are numerous other accounts of big man sightings around the lake, often it's a simple glimpse of one of the hairy beasts darting into the trees and out of sight. Other times, people claim the creatures have come close to their cabins, stealing fish or other food items.

At least one account claims one of the big men took a more aggressive approach.

Attack of the Big Man

Alaskan researcher Ron Wendt relates a strange story from the Iliamna region. The account involves a man named Gus Jensen who was pulled from his bed one night by a hairy creature.

Jensen and his wife were sleeping soundly when something yanked him from bed and started dragging him out of the cabin. The man got wedged across the doorway and the creature began pulling harder, trying to dislodge him. Jensen's shoulder was dislocated in the process.

The delay gave Gus' wife time to grab a rifle and start shooting at the beast. The thing ran away leaving the stunned couple with a weird story to tell.

The Jensen family seems to have had a propensity for run-ins with bigfoot. According to Wendt, Gus' son Vern also had an encounter with the creature.

Vern Jensen and his friend Billy Vaudrin were trapping in the Pedro Bay area when they had their encounter.

The men were using an abandoned cabin for shelter while they were in the area. Locals had told the men to avoid the cabins because they were "bad." The trappers ignored the warnings and picked out the best room of the four-room cabin. They moved a stove into the room for warmth and fixed the broken windows to keep the heat in and the foul weather out.

One night, while the men were sitting in the cabin repairing dog harnesses, they received a shock. Billy Vaudrin looked across the room and saw Jensen's eyes wide with surprise. The man was looking beyond and above, towards the window behind him.

Vaudrin turned in time to see what the man was looking at: a large hairy face peering in the window. The trappers grabbed their guns and rushed outside. Despite how rapidly they responded to the incident, they were unable to capture the creature. Weirdly, no evidence of the beast, tracks or otherwise, was found.

A sighting in the fall of 1998 comes from two men out in Bethel County on September 3rd. The men were sitting on a ridge watching for Caribou. They observed a large, grey bipedal creature emerge from the brush and move along the trees. The men watched the creature for over half an hour. The witness reports:

"We are both long time Alaskans, avid hunters and have logged many, many hunts in North America. I have hunted all of North America's deer, elk, black and grizzly bear. I have never seen an animal like what we saw that day."

The men were in a remote region, forty-five miles (72km) (by air) west of Lake Iliamna in the Mulchantna River Drainage. On their return trip, they told their bush pilot what they had witnessed, and he informed the men they'd likely spotted the "hairy man," known by native people in the Iliamna region.

Lake Iliamna remains a popular spot for fishing and serves as a nursery for the largest red salmon run in the world. Between its mysterious lake monster and tales of big men in the woods surrounding the water, it may be the perfect vacation spot for monster hunters.

Glacial Demon

Time spent in remote regions can be challenging, even for those up to the task. For those unprepared for the starkness of the environment and the lack of community, there are other challenges both mental and emotional.

Early miners and explorers experienced harsh conditions in the search for gold, and as a result, numerous weird tales have come down through history.

At the turn of the century, there was a report of a "glacial demon" in the area around Valdez. Reportedly, the creature or creatures, were hostile and killed at least one man.

Captain W.R. Abercrombie, Second US Infantry, US Army, was sent to Alaska during the Klondike Gold Rush of 1898-1899. Abercrombie was ordered to explore the Valdez and Copper River regions and report his findings to the US War Department.

With the gold rush in full swing, prospectors from all over the world were making the journey with riches on their minds. Many prospectors were traveling via the port of Valdez, making their way to the Dawson area from there.

Captain Abercrombie reached Valdez in April 1899. While at the port, he encountered a group of miners who were in a horrible state of existence. Suffering from scurvy and living in terrible conditions, the men were a reflection of the difficulties of trying to survive in the harsh environment. Abercrombie spent time speaking with the miners, and later made an entry in his journal about what the men called the 'glacial demon.' As he writes:

"I noticed in talking to these people that over seventy per cent of them were more or less mentally deranged. My attention was first directed to this fact by their reference to a 'glacial demon.' One big,

rawboned Swede, in particular, described to me how this demon had strangled his son on the glacier, his story being that he had just started from Twelve-Mile Plant (a small collection of huts just across the Coast Range of Mountains from Valdez) with his son to go to the coast in company with some other prospectors. When halfway up the summit of the glacier, his son, who was ahead of him hauling a sled, while he was behind pushing, called to him, saying that the demon had attacked him and had his arms around his neck. The father ran to the son's assistance, but as he described it, his son being very strong, soon drove the demon away and they passed on their way up toward the summit of Valdez Glacier. The weather was very cold and the wind blowing very hard, so that it made traveling very difficult in passing over the ice between the huge crevasses through which it was necessary to pick their way to gain the summit. While in the thickest of these crevasses, the demon again appeared. He was said to be a small, heavy-built man and very active. He again sprang on the son's shoulders, this time with such a grasp that, although the father did all he could to release him, the demon finally strangled the son to death. The old man then put the son on a sled and brought him down to Twelve-Mile camp, where the other prospectors helped bury him.

During the recital of this tale the old man's eyes would blaze and he would go through all the actions to illustrate just how he fought off this imaginary demon. When I heard this story there were ten or twelve other men in the cabin and at that time it would not have been safe to dispute the theory of the existence of this demon on the Valdez Glacier, as every man there firmly believed it to be a reality."

Abercrombie clearly believed the men were delusional, an assumption that was no doubt easy to reach considering their ragged condition.

But other people have reported strange things around glaciers too.

In 1908, *The Alaska-Yukon Magazine* ran an article about a man who had a weird encounter at the Malaspina Glacier.

The event occurred during the summer a few years prior to publication of the story and involved a prospector named Frank E. Howard. Howard followed the edge of the glacier by canoe until he found a spot to shelter his craft. He got out and set about his explorations. Howard was hoping to reach a rocky ridge he'd seen from the head of Yakutat Bay.

Ice caves near Alaskan glaciers

He donned a set of crampons and started negotiating the perilous glacier, however, part way across, he slipped and fell into a deep crevasse. Luckily, he escaped injury, but he was stuck in a challenging situation; he couldn't climb out the way he had fallen in, so he had to search for other means of escape. He set out following the crevasse, hoping it would lead downhill and eventually open to another route out. As he related to the magazine:

"I was sure the great cavern was crevassed to the surface at some point beyond.

As I kept going ahead, I noticed a gradual increase of light, and in a few more steps, I stood in a broad wall of blue light that came down from above and, looking up, I saw there was no clear opening to the surface. But objects were now revealed some distance around."

Howard was able to make his way out of the crevasse after finding a watercourse that he followed out to a timbered shore.

It was while navigating a path through the crevasse that Howard encountered a weird creature. He described the moment to the magazine:

"Then an object rose slowly out of the glimmer and took form—a spectral thing, with giant form, and lifelike movement. The object rose erect, a goliath in the shape of a man. Then, watching me with a slantwise glance, it walked obliquely from me, until its form faded in the gloom of the cavern.

With its shaggy light-colored fur and huge size, the creature in some ways resembled a bear with bluish gray fur, but that it had a roughly human form, and at all times walked erect."

Whether Howard spotted one of the so-called glacial demons, a sasquatch, or something else altogether remains a mystery.

Whatever it was, it didn't harass him like the things captain Abercrombie had heard about a few years before.

Modern explorers of glacial areas say there are strange things that happen in the ice. Whether it's a result of some unknown effect on the human mind, or whether the areas are the domain of undiscovered creatures remains to be seen.

The Strange Tale of Harry D. Colp

One of the most unusual stories involving weird creatures in Alaska is the tale of gold prospector Harry D. Colp.

Colp's handwritten manuscript was discovered by his family and fell into the hands of his daughter, Virginia. She published the account in 1953 under the title *"The Strangest Story Ever Told."* The weird tale has remained popular over the years, going through, at last count, nine editions.

Virginia gives a note on the tale's background in the preface:

"The writer of this story has been dead for several years now. At one time, back in the early thirties, he had this story written up ready to send away. Something happened, and the manuscript was put into a box and forgotten. During the years the Devil's Country story had been passed along by word of mouth so often that the details had become obscured. It was then a very pleasant surprise when Mother found the manuscript just a short time ago and gave it to me to read. I found it fascinating and I was left with a feeling of curiosity. I wonder if any of you readers will be curious—I wonder—Well, I'll just let you wonder."

Harry Colp's account is a personal one, a documentation of his experiences beginning in the spring of 1900 when he and three companions were in Wrangell. The four men were prospectors, and at the time, they were flat broke and looking for potential ways to strike it rich.

Colp uses pseudonyms for the other men, dubbing them John, Charlie and Fred. He details their experiences as they learn about a potential gold-rich spot in the Thomas Bay area. Excited about the prospect of a mining claim, the men agree to send one of their number on an expedition to survey the area while the others prepared supplies. Charlie is elected and sets out in May with three month's supplies. The remaining men work in Wrangell to save money and prepare for the coming mining efforts.

They're shocked when Charlie returns in early June, far sooner than expected. He presents the men with a chunk of quartz riddled with gold flecks, an indication of a rich vein of gold.

The prospectors are very excited about the quartz and are anxious for a full report, but it doesn't come right away. Charlie it seems, is a changed man. He says little about his trip and goes to sleep, clearly exhausted from the journey.

It's late the next afternoon before the anxious miners finally get the full story from Charlie. It's not what they expect. Before he relates the full account of his time in Thomas Bay, he makes a request of his friends:

"Fellows, the SS Drigo will be in on her way south early tomorrow morning. Can you give me enough money for my ticket to Seattle? I'm through with Alaska and never want to see it again. I'll tell you about my trip to Thomas Bay and where I found that quartz but my advice to you is to forget about it. It will never do you any good…"

After a commitment from the other three men, and a promise that his real name would not be used, the man proceeded to recount the details of his experience in Thomas Bay.

Charlie gave a full accounting, including details of the points he had stopped at, where he camped and even weather conditions. He gave them men clear details regarding where he discovered the gold-flecked piece of quartz.

According to Charlie's tale, he was initially excited about the gold prospects in the region he was exploring. He was anxious to gather more details and get back to his friends so they could return to the spot and start mining operations. But his excitement didn't last.

As Charlie set about getting his bearings and making a careful study of landmarks and positions, his explorations took a disturbing turn. Colp relates the incident that Charlie described:

"Right there, fellows, I got the scare of my life. I hope to God I never see or go through the likes of it again. Swarming up the ridge toward me from the lake were the most hideous creatures. I couldn't call them anything but devils, as they were neither men nor monkeys — yet looked like both. They were entirely sexless, their bodies covered with long coarse hair, except where the scabs and running sores had replaced it. Each one seemed to be reaching out for me and striving to be the first to get me. The air was full of their cries and the stench from their sores and bodies made me faint.

I forgot my broken gun and tried to use it on the first ones, then I threw it at them and turned and ran. God, how I did run! I could feel their hot breath on my back. Their long claw like fingers scraped my back. The smell from their steaming, stinking bodies was making me sick; while the noises they made, yelling, screaming and breathing, drove me mad. Reason left me. How I reached the canoe or how I hung on to that piece of quartz is a mystery to me."

After his harrowing escape from the strange creatures, Charlie woke that night and found himself in the bottom of his boat, drifting somewhere between Thomas Bay and Sukoi Island. Once he was fully conscious, he started making his way to Wrangell and traveled until he was able to rejoin his friends.

The men were of course stunned by the tale and found it difficult to reconcile the account. For his part, the only thing on Charlie's mind was leaving. He concluded:

"You no doubt think I am either crazy or lying, all I can say is… never let me hear the name of Thomas Bay again, and for God's sake, help me get away tomorrow on that boat!"

Colp's book goes on to describe other strange incidents in what is called the "Devil's Country," but Charlie's account stands out as one of particular interest for those interested in cryptids.

What did the man encounter on his expedition? Some speculate that the creatures were related to sasquatch, but there are startling differences between what Charlie recounted and other sasquatch tales.

The fact that there were a group of the creatures, combined with their clearly unhealthy condition leaves many questions lingering.

Something wholly unique may have been lurking around Thomas Bay. Thomas Bay itself has a reputation for misfortunes. Located in the southeast portion of the state, the area suffered a massive landslide in 1750 after which it acquired the nickname "The Bay of Death."

There's been some speculation that the creatures in the area are connected to the infamous *Koushtaka*.

Harry Colp himself had strange experiences in the Thomas Bay region, recounted in his book, but outside of his writing, he never publicly spoke about the incidents or Charlie's story.

Other scattered tales about the region surfaced over the years. In 1925, a trapper reportedly found strange tracks in the area. Described as a cross between a bear's and a human's footprints, the trapper's dog vanished under mysterious circumstances.

Checking on his traps, he found some had been sprung though they were empty, and others had been destroyed. The man set off to search for his dog and was never heard from again.

In a 1974 interview, Virginia stated she was positive of the veracity of her father's account, but she couldn't say whether or not it was all fact.

The mystery of the strange little creatures in the Devil's Country remains a curious puzzle.

Harry D. Colp's original handwritten manuscript is now kept at the Alaska State Library in Juneau.

The Mystery of Port Chatham

In 2016 *Alaska Magazine* ran a brief story under the headline:

"Something's Afoot in Port Chatham—Century-old Rumors Persist of a Terror in the Mountains."

As noted in the headline, the tale has been told for a century, but the mystery remains to this day. It's a tale that involves a small village on the bay at Port Chatham, and rumors of a deadly creature responsible for frightening residents out of the area.

Port Chatham is a bay on the southern tip of the Kenai Peninsula. The town in question, known as both Portlock and Port Chatham, is now a ghost town and legend says the reason for its abandonment was the presence of a monstrous creature in the surrounding hills, one that preyed on the community's residents.

In the early 20th century, Portlock was an active cannery community. Named after Captain Nathaniel Portlock of the Royal Navy, natives had lived in the area well before the United States took control of Alaska. In 1921, a post office opened in the town, officially putting it on the map. The community first appeared on the U.S. Census in 1940 when the unincorporated village listed a total of 31 residents. The bulk of them were working for the canning industry.

Whether due to its remote location, or other factors, the small town never really grew and by 1950, the Post Office closed. The community was officially dissolved as a CDP (Census Designated Place) after the 1980 census.

The mystery surrounding the town predates government statistics. Disturbing incidents in the area go back to at least the 1930s.

The first notable recorded incident was in 1931 when a logger named Andrew Kamluck was found dead in the woods. He had been killed by a blow to the head. Curiously, it's speculated the "weapon" used was a large piece of log-moving equipment. Not something a human would be capable of picking up and swinging about.

Around the time of Kamluck's murder, a local prospector set out into the hills for a day of gold mining. The man vanished and no sign of him was ever found.

The incidents could of course be put down to accidents or human activity, but things became stranger a short time later when another man saw a frightening creature.

Tom Larsen was out chopping wood for his fish traps when he spotted something large and hairy on the beach. Larsen rushed to his home and retrieved a rifle. When he returned to the spot, the creature was still there at the water's edge. Larsen claimed the thing stood up and stared at him. For reasons unknown, Larsen never fired at the beast.

The tale of the abandoned town took another turn in 1973 when news reports began to talk about the mystery. A story published in the April 15, 1973 edition of the *Anchorage Daily News*, gives us some of the details:

"Portlock began its existence sometime after the turn of the century, as a cannery town. In 1921 a post office was established here, and for a time the residents, mostly natives of Russian-Aleut extraction, lived in peace with their picturesque mountain-and-sea setting.

Then, sometime in the beginning years of World War II, rumors began to seep along the Kenai Peninsula that things were not right in Portlock. Men from the cannery town would go up into the hills to hunt the Dall sheep and bear, and never return. Worse yet, the stories ran, sometimes their mutilated bodies would be swept down into the lagoon, torn and dismembered in a way that bears could not, or would not, do.

Tales were told of villagers tracking moose over soft ground. They would find giant, man-like tracks over 18 inches (46cm) in length closing upon those of the moose, the signs of a short struggle where the grass had been matted down, then only the deep tracks of the manlike animal departing toward the high, fog-shrouded mountains with their deep valleys and hidden glaciers."

Was a giant, vicious beast hiding in the country around the community? Some believed this was the case and that no one was safe.

More was revealed years later in the October 2009 edition of the *Homer Tribune*. Reporter Naomi Klouda interviewed an elder born in Port Chatham in 1934. The woman recalled her memories of the incidents that led to her family fleeing the town.

Malania Helen Kehl said her family was terrorized for "a long period of time" before they and the other villagers left the community. Kehl's family moved to Nanwalek after leaving Port Chatham.

"We left our houses and the school and started all new here."

Kehl recounts that residents of the village wouldn't go into the surrounding mountains and forests since it was too dangerous. They were so fearful of the creature that it drove them *en masse* out of their community.

The creature, Kehl said, was a *"Nantiinaq,"* (nan-te-nuk), or "Big, Hairy man," a legendary and frightening figure described as being half-man and half-beast.

Today, Portlock/Port Chatham remains a ghost town. The area is difficult to access and while some Alaskan publications state the area is accessible by ATVs, locals say that's not the case. The only way to reach the area is via bush plane or boat. Little remains of the former community and residents of nearby towns say the area is haunted and dangerous.

In 2010, a naturalist interpreter named Brad Josephs spent two weeks interviewing elders in the village of Nanwalek. Josephs, a resident of Homer, learned much about native views of the hairy creature and its varied forms.

According to information gathered from his contacts, the creature can take on an animal form similar to a bear on two feet, but it is also acknowledged as a powerful spirit.

Natives in the region also believe that when a village is interfering with the environment, the creature will make its presence known, a natural response from something connected to the land, warning people of the imbalance.

The concept may sound far too mystical for those seeking a flesh and blood undiscovered animal, but it's important to realize that native cultures view such things through the lens of cultural traditions and worldview.

Stories of physical encounters with the creatures are not cancelled out by the concept of mystical connections associated with the beasts, rather, all aspects are looked at in a perspective that encompasses practicality as well as spirituality.

The villagers may have left the cursed town, but stories of the Hairy Men in the region are still prominent at the deserted village, as well as near their new community.

Brad Josephs heard an account from the region that involved a forestry crew working on a field management program. While spending the night near a chain of lakes in the area, the crew heard "wild screaming and trees crashing down."

The crew rushed back into town to get help. Several native men went back to the area with the crew and they too heard screams and "ape-like yells" in the area.

Other people have reported hearing the weird screams described as something similar to Howler monkeys, but much deeper in tone and longer in duration.

Whatever made the sounds remained hidden in the forest.

Another account comes from a family out fishing in the area. The father spotted a large, hairy bipedal thing standing at the edge of the water. The creature was seven feet (2.1m) tall, and the stunned fisherman watched as the beast made eye contact with him before turning and vanishing into the trees.

There are other stories from the area too. A lone man hunting in the region in 1968 reported being chased by a strange creature while on the trail of goats.

Ed Schlief, owner of Alaska Bowhunting Supply in Anchorage, believes he had an encounter with the creature in

August 1973. At the time, Schlief and two friends were on a hunting trip on the southwestern end of the Kenai Peninsula.

A storm came up and the men were forced up into Dogfish Bay to weather it out. They set up camp, pitched a canvas tent, and had a dinner of salmon. The group carefully cleaned everything to deter bears coming into the camp, then turned in for the night. At two a.m., Ed was roused by one of his fellow hunters. Something was outside their tent.

All three men sat awake and listened. Whatever it was, it moved in a slow and deliberate fashion, circling their tent. None of the men ventured out to see what had intruded into their camp.

The next morning, no tracks were found, and the trio continued with their day. More foul weather kept the crew in the same location the following night, and once again they were roused by the sound of footsteps circling the tent. On this occasion, they got up the nerve to shine flashlights outside the tent, but they were not able to spot the creature that had been exploring their camp.

Years later in 1990, Ed Schlief was working as a paramedic when he heard another account. Ed and his partner were transporting an elderly man to the Native Hospital in Anchorage. As it turned out, the patient was an Aleut from Port Graham. Schlief made reference to once being caught in a storm near Port Graham and having to camp out until it passed. Suddenly, the elderly Aleut sat up, grabbed Ed's shirt and said:

"Did it bother you?"

Taken aback, Schlief said the hair stood up on the back of his neck and he responded to the man with a quick *"Yes!"*

The Aleut excitedly asked his next question:

"Did you see it?"

"No," Schlief responded, *"but my brother seen it! It chased him!"*

According to Schlief:

"This old Aleut and I were talking about the same thing, but we

never used the word bigfoot or hairy man or anything like that. But we both knew what we were talking about."

Today, accounts of Hairy Men continue to come out of the region. Whatever the truth behind the legend of Portlock/Port Chatham, people mostly avoid the area and tales of curses and dangerous creatures still abound.

Whatever ran people out of the village all those years ago continues to hold dominance over the region.

Land of the Otter Men

When it comes to Alaskan cryptids, one of the most difficult topics to approach is that of the *Kushtaka*, or, "land otter men."

Some modern researchers believe that tales of the creatures represent another guise of sasquatch, but leaping to this conclusion simplifies the topic and ignores the First Nations view. In fact, members of Native Alaskan tribes strongly disagree with the assessment that a *Kushtaka* is a bigfoot, pointing out they have other names for the familiar hairy giant.

The *Kushtaka* is found in both Tlingit and Tsimshian lore of southeastern Alaska. The creatures are shapeshifters, able to take human form, or the form of an otter. Often, they are described as something in between. A bipedal creature half human and half otter.

There are reportedly between six and eight feet (1.8 – 2.4m) in height. Covered in sleek, black or dark brown fur. They have human-like hands, but they have talons on their fingers. Their feet are like a human's. Their eyes are large, and by some accounts, the eyes glow. Their mouths are full of needlelike teeth and they have a long tail. They emit a high pitched, three-part whistle in the pattern of low-high-low.

The creatures have a vast range of supernatural powers. It's said they prey on small children and purportedly, the creatures can even take the full form of other humans or use the voice of a target's friends and relatives to attract their attention.

Some consider the term itself taboo and believe that even mentioning the creatures attracts their attention. It's a belief found in other cultures around the world in connection to supernatural entities. In the Middle East, mention of the infamous djinn attracts their unwanted attention. In the

American Southwest, the term skinwalker is equally considered a word best not used least you draw them to you.

Historians and folklorists think the *Kushtaka* was a type of bogeyman used by Tlingit mothers to scare their children into following the rules. But casting the creature in the guise of a folkloric or mythical entity doesn't address the serious nature with which First Nations people view the topic. And the *Kushtaka* is a very serious matter. It's a topic that weaves through the physical and magical worlds of native culture. The threat is real, and whether it's ultimately a metaphor or the lore of a real physical being almost becomes irrelevant.

Early Tales

There are many traditional tales related to the *Kushtaka*. Frederica de Laguna relates an account of someone captured by the creatures:

"My father's oldest brother got captured by land otters out at Situk. He was about four years old. My mother told us, 'Don't go too far in the dark, in the nighttime'…He was found two days later, caught between the roots of a tree. When he came to, it was dark, pouring down rain, and he had no clothes on or anything…That Indian doctor's spirit caught him. He got under the trees. The kucda-qa dragged him through the roots. They let him drop right between them. He pooped all over himself and they don't want to handle him…"

Some traditional tales relate that even if someone survives being captured by the *Kushtaka* and escapes, they are never the same and may even go insane from the experience. De Laguna gives us an example of such stories, writing about a girl who was taken but returned:

"The girl had encountered Land Otter Men in the woods and returned half-crazed and raging, she attacked everyone, struck and bit those who tried to hold her, and tearing off her clothes, ran around naked…"

A May 19, 1994 article in the *Petersburg Pilot* gives us details of a *Kushtaka* encounter from the 1930s. The incident involved a Tlingit hunter and occurred in the infamous "Devils Country" of Thomas Bay.

The man was deep in the woods when he heard a strange whistling sound followed by someone calling his name. A weird feeling overtook him, and he realized that a *Kushtaka* was nearby attempting to lure him away. Following an old tradition, the man grabbed a branch and bit down hard on the wood. He gathered his strength and quickly left the area. It's said the man was so disturbed by his experience that he never hunted again.

Why the Otter?

A curious question arises when studying the lore of the *Kushtaka*. Out of all of Alaska's animals, why the otter?

Why indeed. Normally, at least in the modern view, otters are perceived as joyous and happy animals. They're sociable creatures and are both playful and industrious. American naturalist Ernest Thompson Seton wrote of the otter:

"...the joyful, keen and fearless otter; mild and loving to his own kind, and gentle with his neighbor of the stream; full of play and gladness in his life, full of courage in his stress; ideal in his home, steadfast in death; the noblest little soul that ever went four-footed through the woods."

Yet, in the history of some Alaskan First Nations people, otters became the form taken by a strange otherworldly, and rather dark creature, the *Kushtaka*.

Anthropologist Richard Barazzuol offers some insight on why the animal may have come to be connected to such a dark aspect. His study of Tlingit beliefs regarding otters was detailed in his thesis *The Tlingit Land Otter Complex: Coherence in the Social and Shamanic Order*. Barazzuol writes:

"The sea otter had a prestigious place in Tlingit society as a bringer of wealth during the period of the fur trade until its near extinction in the nineteenth century. However, it is the land otter that occupied a prominent place in the belief systems of the Tlingit. The land otter was probably perceived as the most human-like animal in that environment.

Particular attributes of the land otters lead to the perception that it has the ability to create a symbolic bridge uniting human and animal. It was seen as an ambiguous figure which had the ability, like the Tlingit themselves, to function well both on the land and in the water."

The concept that Barazzuol mentions, and the human-like behavior of otters, likely went a long way in the native belief of the *Kushtaka*, a creature that represents something truly in between.

Shamanic Perspectives

Mary Giraudo Beck mentions the shamanic view of the *Kushtaka* and reminds us of the shaman's role in Alaskan culture. As a mediator between the world of human beings and the world of supernatural entities, the shaman could travel between the two realms of existence. When possible, the shaman could save those captured by the *Kushtaka*, bringing them back to the world of normal human existence. Beck reports on the role of the *Kushtaka*:

"Kushtakas were human beings who had been transformed by land otters into creatures similar to themselves, but who retained some human qualities. They kidnapped children, frightened women, and caused storms, avalanches, disease, and famine. Kushtakas had been given their dual role by Raven, when he bestowed on land otters the gifts of being able to live both on land and under the water as well as powers of illusion and disguise. In addition, he gave them the special mission of saving those lost at sea or in the woods and transforming them into half-human, half-otter beings like themselves."

Beck brings up an important aspect of the *Kushtaka* and its relationship with the people. Namely, that the *Kushtaka* were once humans.

Let's be clear, some accounts claim the *Kushtaka* kill humans in a terrible manner, namely, by using their claws and teeth to rip victims to pieces. But as with many First Nations concepts, it's never so simple.

The *Kushtaka*, in a strange way, can sometimes be helpful. Those who are lost in the wilderness, or those who are drowning may be saved by one of the creatures. There's a catch of course, being saved by a *Kushtaka* means being transformed into one. The transformation allows the human to survive cold temperatures or frigid waters.

The exact process of the transformation is shrouded in mystery. It's said that the *Kushtaka* creates illusions of the person's family and friends to distract them while the change takes place. As the physical transformation begins, the person slowly turns into a hybrid creature more otter than human.

While the transformation allows the victim to survive, it's more of a curse than a blessing. They are never the same, never able to return to their homes or their families, and they are forever trapped in the form of a shapeshifting beast.

The only hope for a human caught in the process of being transformed into a *Kushtaka* is that someone, a normal human, would recognize them. Such an acknowledgement could pull one back from the brink before it was too late.

Most Tlingit consider the idea of being turned into one of the otter people terrifying. By the nation's traditions, one must die a human in order to achieve reincarnation and find peace in the hereafter. Unless a tribal shaman is able to undo the damage done, a human transformed into a *Kushtaka* is forever lost.

The importance of proper passage and preparation for the afterlife is reflected in the Tlingit treatment of the dead. From the Tlingit perspective, death was one thing, but an unrecovered corpse could lead to horrors beyond imagining. Without proper ceremonial care, the soul could not transition and would not have the opportunity to reincarnate back into the clan's lineage.

Those lost in blizzards or drowned in the ocean represented a problem for the tribal system. Were they really lost, or had they been claimed by the supernatural *Kushtaka*?

Reportedly, land otters take victims deep into dens, often built along the riverbanks. There the victim is further enchanted into believing he has made it home, at least, until the full transformation has been completed.

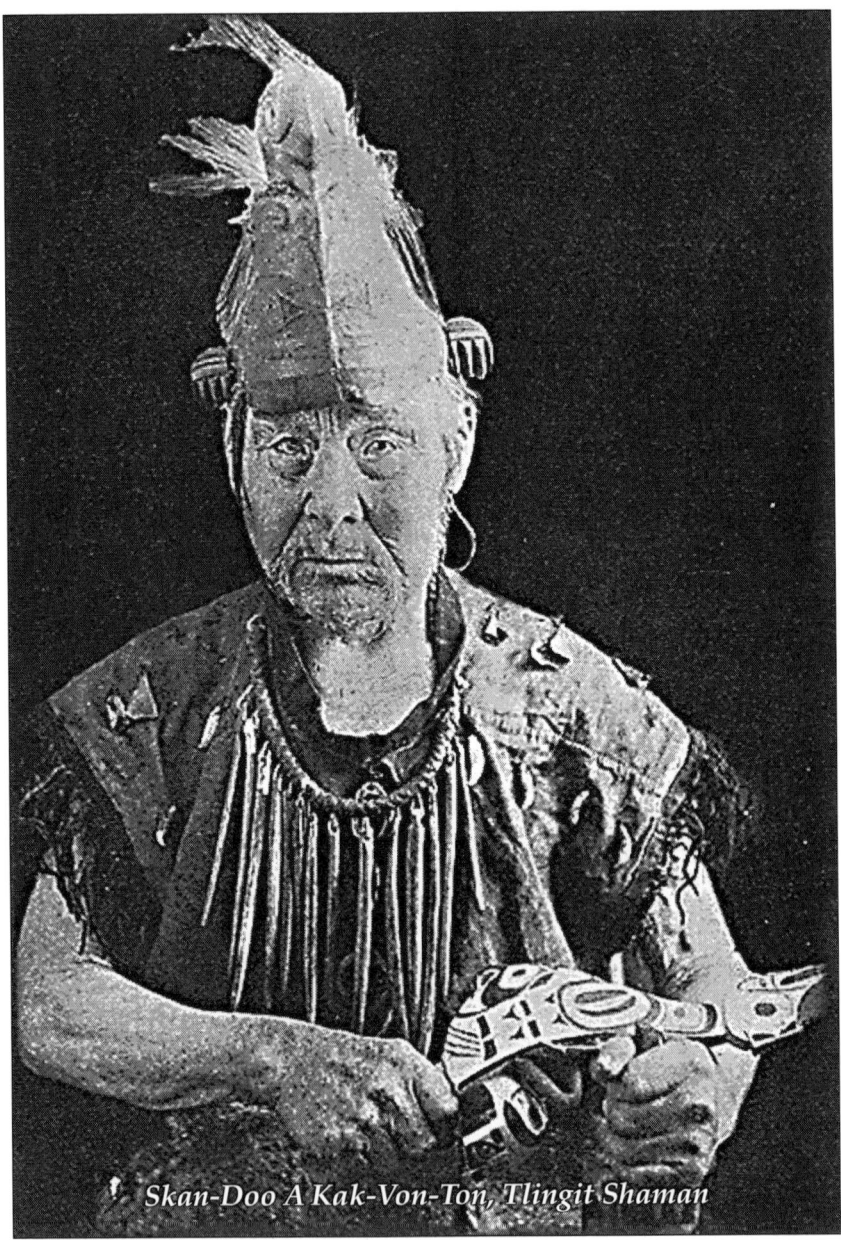

Skan-Doo A Kak-Von-Ton, Tlingit Shaman

De Laguna writes that *Kushtaka* actively hunt victims. They have the ability to not only shape-shift, but to hypnotize and to drive people insane. The writer also makes note of the *Kushtaka* ability to mimic the sound of a baby crying, or the scream of a woman. Whenever a child went missing, the *Kushtaka* were suspected, but hunters and those out on the water were vulnerable too.

"They (Land Otter Men) appear to him (victim) in the guise of his own relatives or friends, and the place to which they take him looks just like his own house. Here they offer him some of their food. But if he eats it, he can never come back to his own home again. He will go 'crazy' and become a land otter."

De Laguna seems to have gone a step further in his report, adding the danger of eating food in the land of the *Kushtaka*, a concept in line with European fairy lore.

Explorers who had early contact with Alaskan peoples listened to tales of the *Kushtaka* and heard these views expressed by the people themselves. An excellent example comes from George Thornton Emmons.

Emmons was a US Navy lieutenant stationed in Alaska during the late 1800s. He wrote extensively of Tlingit culture. Toward the end of his life, at the request of the American Museum of Natural History, Emmons began organizing decades of ethnographic notes. After his death, Frederica de Laguna spent 30 additional years editing Emmons's material before his respected book, *The Tlingit Indians*, was published in 1991. He wrote about the *Kushtaka* and the spiritual threat of unrecovered bodies:

"Since cremation was not only a religious rite but a sacred duty, necessary to the happiness of the dead, drowning and the loss of the body was the most dreaded death. The body of the drowned, if not recovered, might be 'rescued' by the Land Otter People and would become a Koushta ka, or Land Otter Man. The transformation was slowly accomplished: first hair grew over the body, speech became confused, he began to walk on knees and elbows, a tail grew out, and, in time, he became more otter than human. Upon seeing anyone, he would try to be recognized and if so, he would be saved. If his body was found and cremated, he would be saved."

It's important to note that humans who did manage to survive the transformation, or who escaped from the land of the

157

otter people and were brought back to the land of humans were considered a prime candidate to become a shaman themselves. Having tread into such dangerous territory, another world essentially, they were seen as gifted or empowered and would hopefully be able to further empower the people by taking on a shamanic role with the benefit of added knowledge of the world of the otter people.

Long Tail People

In her book, *Ghosts of Alaska*, Jody Ellis-Knapp mentions what she calls the "Long Tail people." Jody says she heard stories of the creatures from family members:

"No one speaks much of the Long Tail people. My uncle told me a few stories but said if you asked a Native Alaskan about them, they are reluctant to speak of it. The stories seem to originate in the Copper River area, but no one seems to know from where exactly. There is a bad feeling associated with this creature. Some believe that talking too much about an entity or creature will invite it into your world, and from the description of the Long Tails, no one wants them coming to dinner."

During my time in Alaska, I've asked a number of people about the "Long Tail men." The usual responses vary from a shake of the head in the negative, or an indication that the stories are related to accounts of the *Kushtaka*.

Accounts of the Long Tail people tend towards the gruesome. Reportedly, the creatures live, or previously lived, under the banks of rivers, deep in the mud. Their underground lairs were accessible via caves and holes along the riverbanks.

The creepiest aspect of the Long Tail people has to do with their diet—reportedly, their preferred sustenance is human flesh.

Although not as intelligent as humans, the Long Tails are supposed to have tribal structure with leaders. They are most active at twilight but are rarely seen since they are adept at camouflaging themselves.

Accounts of the Long Tail men are scarce, but there is one historic report. It involves a battle between a group of Long

Tail men and some First Nations warriors in the Copper River region.

The account was reported by Reverend Arthur R. Wright, a missionary in Alaska in the early 1900s.

Wright was half native, being born to a white father and an Athabaskan mother. He was educated by the church and became a missionary, spending much time among the people from his mother's side of the family.

In 1924, Reverend Wright recounted a story about the Long Tail men that he heard while in the Copper River area. His account was published in the February 7th edition of the *Cordova Daily News*:

"On a recent trip over to the Copper River the Indians drew my attention to numerous holes in an embankment we passed. On inquiring of them I was told that those were the holes of 'men with tails.' With some questioning, this is the tale I heard.

In the Selina River country were rolling hills on which numerous caribou roamed. The Indians who subsisted on meat were lured to this district by the abundance of game. And years ago, at the mouth of the Selina River they built a large Indian village.

One day a dog brought into the camp the tail of a fish. No one had caught any fish, and it puzzled the Indians as to how the animal got the fish. Finally, it was decided to search the district to determine if there were any other tribes in the area.

A group went out to search for the unknown people. When several of the searchers did not return, the tribe knew something was wrong.

What had happened to these men?

Finally, one of their most skilled trackers was sent in search of the missing scouts.

He made his way cautiously through the country. At length he came upon a hidden trail through the woods. Across the path at intervals was stretched a rope made of grass. This he examined very carefully.

'A trap...an alarm,' he thought.

He continued to follow the trail, which led to a group of caves he could see in the distance.

Very cautiously he strained eye and ear for sight or sound of anything unusual. Finally, from out of the numerous caves came men with tails. They had all the appearance of normal men except for a tail, which dragged behind them. He was much surprised to see them use these tails as their chief means of locomotion. They curled their tails forward between their legs and recoiled in such a manner as to push themselves forward.

As the scout watched them, keeping to windward to avoid being detected by scent, they kicked what looked to him like a ball. On observing it more closely, the Indian recognized to his horror the head of one of his companions.

He watched them rush to and fro, capering about with much shouting and hideous glee, evidently having a game of ball with the head.

He quickly noted their number, also the number of caves, and returned back to his camp.

After he made his report, a group of men and boys gathered, and an attack was planned on the village of Tail Men. They decided to seal off the caves with fire and smoke, thus killing the people inside.

It was raining when they reached the caves and the Tail Men were all inside. Each group was detailed to a cave. With burning brands and brush, the Indians rushed the caves and plugged the openings.

As the attackers stood guard, through the fire came flights of arrows. Soon this stopped. After all signs of life from the Tail Men had ceased, the Indians returned homeward.

The Tail Men were no more a menace to the Indians. Today all that remains of them are this legend, their caves, and numerous arrowheads.

Thus, ended the story, and someday I hope to return and try to find out more about these Tail Men."

It's unclear whether Reverend Wright ever went back to the area to learn more about the Tail Men since nothing else has turned up on record.

Modern Views

The wilds of Southeast Alaska are beautiful. Lush, green woods, abundant wildlife and plenty of fresh water. The natural beauty doesn't prevent the strangeness of the tales that come from the region. There's an unsettling quality when considering the *Kushtaka* and the world it thrives in. It's as if the richness of the environment itself is a lure the creature uses.

Many people who never see one of the creatures report odd experiences in the woods that could be explained by the otter men. Tales of odd feelings, sudden compulsions, hallucinations and more. Some people report hearing familiar voices and other sounds they can't explain. Whether the experiences can be attributed to some unknown natural phenomenon or whether it's part and parcel of supernatural beings in the wild remains to be seen.

What is known, is that there are people who say the *Kushtaka* are still out there, still being encountered, still a danger.

One Alaskan told me there have been numerous accounts of *Kushtaka* around the city of Haines. Reportedly, they have been seen at several locations on the outskirts of the city and in broad daylight. Fear of the creatures made him reluctant to share his personal account, though he did note that he didn't believe talking about them a little would put him in danger.

A man I met in southeast Alaska spoke briefly about the topic. He didn't have a personal account, but several secondhand stories. He did have some comments about the native reluctance to even speak about the creatures:

"It's a funny thing because some people want to dismiss it and say it's just superstition, but no, there's something very real about it, about the topic. Now, I don't think I'm superstitious and my wife, she's Tlingit but she went to college and is a professional, you wouldn't call her superstitious either. But there are some things, some of the old ways, that she still holds to. You don't bring those things up around her or her family. They say that speaking that name is bad luck. I don't talk about it with them, I don't want to offend them, but I guess part of me wonders how real it is. Why take the chance I guess?"

A man I interviewed in Ketchikan was a bit more direct

when I interviewed him. He was sure he and his brother had experienced a close call with a *Kushtaka* and he was willing to tell his story. The pair were camping in the summer of 2001 when the incident occurred. The specific location is withheld by his request.

"My brother came home for a visit and we hadn't seen each other in quite a while, so we took off to camp for a couple of days, just like old times for us. Our family was living further down south at the time and there were plenty of places that we liked to go...anyway, we set up camp one night and settled in, just talking and catching up. That's when we heard it, the whistling. High pitched and in a pattern, low then high then low, just like the old stories say.

It was moving around us, first behind us, then a few minutes later, over on the side. We were getting pretty nervous cause they can turn you, make you one of them if they get hold of you. I started feeling real funny with a light head. Then it was on the other side. We grabbed our stuff, ready to get out of there and we stood up looking around trying to figure out where it was. Through the trees on one side, we saw something very tall moving. We only caught a glimpse of it, it was behind the trees. It was on two legs and tall, at least six or seven feet (1.8 – 2.1m) and what we did catch a sight of was a long tail trailing behind it.

We got out and never went back to that spot. Our grandfather said it was one of them."

With so much fear surrounding the creatures, the question arises, what is one to do if confronted with one of the otter people?

Ironically, as dangerous as they are thought to be, native tradition says they shouldn't be killed. As J. Robert Alley writes:

"Killing a kushtakaa was expressly forbidden as it may likely have been a lost relative, or since killing one might have incited a war with the kushtakaas. Of all Native people in southeast Alaska, the Tlingit especially have continued to carry a strong regard for leaving such creatures alone, and would certainly take issue with anyone inclined toward shooting such a being, although such Native events are occasionally referred to among the northern Tlingit."

Despite this belief, there's nothing that says people should simply give in to the creatures. According to old traditions, there are several things that can be used to ward the *Kushtaka* off. Urine is one of the primary defenses against the *Kushtaka*. Additionally, Copper, fire and tobacco are all said to be useful in keeping the creatures at bay.

Dogs are perhaps the best defense against the *kushtaka*. It's said the barking of a dog can force the creatures to reveal themselves. The creatures are afraid of dogs since dogs can kill them. In some cases, the bones of dogs are considered a protective talisman against the shapeshifters.

The *Kushtaka* are a unique creature, even by Alaskan standards and although tales have become more widespread in modern times, the otter people are firmly based in the traditions of only a portion of the state's native population.

J. Robert Alley says the Haida have tales of a creature similar to the *Kushtaka*, one they call *"Gagiit."* Roughly translated, the term means "man on all fours." While *Gagiit* tales seem more akin to classic wild man accounts, the Haida believe those lost at sea or in the wilderness are often transformed into *Gagiit*.

Overall, the Haida accounts could represent a curious blend of wild man stories and Tlingit lore of the otter men.

A Haida man told Alley that the creatures were known to make vocalizations and his people were well aware they were dangerous.

"I don't think there's a hunter in Hydaburg, who if he were in the bush and heard the sound of a baby crying, wouldn't turn around and head right back the other way!"

Modern times have brought changing views of the monster. Bjorn Dihle discusses the otter people in his book Haunted Inside Passage, and he includes an interesting passage about today's take on the creatures. Dihle heard a unique perspective from native speaker David Katzeek, who told him:

"There's all kind of Kooshdaa Kaas. You're going to find it in resentment. Anger. Ego. Self-esteem will be part of it...It's causing people to destroy the earth. If you see what people are doing to people. How they're treating other people because they don't look like them,

talk like them, walk like them…That's the spirit of Kooshdaa Kaa."

Katzeek goes further, stating that the tales may be ancient, but their message is very relevant even today:

"Every human being has a Kooshdaa Kaa in him. This is not modern stuff I'm telling you. This is the ancient kind of stuff that the elders would bring to the table. That's the reason why I'm saying the elders, if they were sitting here, they would be nodding their heads up and down because all the stories have it in it. Here is the thing they wanted everyone to know: that there is a Kooshdaa Kaa and it does take possession of you. It can actually take possession of your soul."

When it comes down to it, the *Kushtaka* is a concept that, more often than not, eludes understanding from a westernized perspective.

If it is a physical creature, a cryptid if you will, then it is also much, much more. It is a form, a defined manifestation of something that lies beyond, just out of reach of rational comprehension. A monster, a supernatural entity and an unknowable force that can overtake one without warning.

In many ways, the *Kushtaka* is a perfect reflection of the stark beauty and sheer deadliness of the wilds of Alaska. It's sometimes what you think, never what you expect, and always a tangible presence one must come to terms with while walking the snowy landscape of the last frontier.

*A note on spelling:

There are numerous spelling variations for the creatures being discussed here. Kooshdaa Kaa, Koushtaka, Kooshdakhaa and more. There's controversy over the proper form and the reluctance of native speakers to even talk about the topic doesn't make it a simple matter. Therefore, for simplicity's sake, and with all due respect to native speakers, I have elected to use one of the most common variations, *Kushtaka* unless quoting a text where I have left the form used intact.

PART THREE
Strange Survivors, Lost Species & Other Legends

Raven totem

Thunderbirds

Thunderbirds. Some say they're purely mythical creatures, legends drawn from the lore of various North American tribal cultures.

Others believe stories of the creatures are some kind of primal memory, drawn from a time when our ancestors saw large creatures in the skies above.

For cryptozoologists, the term represents a curious puzzle. A puzzle created by witness accounts of massive winged creatures seen in the sky at various locations. Some of these "birds" are prehistoric in appearance and those who report them believe they've witnessed something impossible, something from the age of dinosaurs. Others appear to be normal, feathered birds. Normal with the exception of their size. Some who have seen these giant birds say they're the size of small airplanes.

Native Legends

The lore of Alaskan First Nations people is rich with tales of thunderbirds. Traditionally, the creatures are supernatural beings with a range of powers, often connected to storms.

Tlingit tradition has long spoken of a massive bird that once dominated the skies over their lands. When it flew, the bird created storms, the flapping of its wings causing thunder to boom, and lightning shot from its eyes when it blinked. The massive bird fed on whales but was also known to take humans.

James Swanton, who spent time studying the traditions of the Tlingit, noted their association of the thunderbird with rain, thunder and lightning. He wrote:

"The thunder bird [sic] keeps on thundering and the sky continues cloudy until the bird catches a whale. Then it carries the whale up into

the mountains, where bones of whales caught in the summer may often be seen. A hunter from Daxe't was once overtaken by a thunderstorm and was blinded by a great flash. When he finally looked up, he saw a big thunder bird astride of a mountain. It had the general appearance of an eagle. Another time some Sitka people out in a choppy place in the ocean heard thundering going on in a certain direction and, repairing to that point next day, found a whale lodged in the trees with claw marks on it. A Russian vessel was almost carried away by one of these birds because the sailors had made fun of it."

William H. Dall also recorded Tlingit knowledge of the thunderbird in the Alaskan panhandle, including the story of the bird *Kunna-kat-eth* at home on Mount Edgecumbe, opposite Sitka.

The Tlingit also say thunderbirds lived in a glacier near Katalla and reportedly they had seen massive feathers as well as whale bones at the location.

Knowledge of thunderbirds extended to the Inuit, or Eskimos, as well. Henry Rink, in his collection of Eskimo traditions, mentions the tribe's knowledge of *"Serdlemaks,"* which were "fabulous birds."

Edward W.Nelson also recorded an Eskimo story of the "last of the Thunderbirds (*Mu-Tugh-O-Wik*)" from along the lower Yukon River.

According to the story, giant eagles had lived in the mountains, but they declined in numbers until only one pair remained nested on a mountain near Sabotnisky. (In 1899, Sabotnisky was a native village on the right bank of the Yukon River, near present day Fortuna Ledge).

The giant birds preyed on reindeer as well as humans who were carried off to the mountain nest to be eaten. The birds sealed their fate one summer day when they made off with the wife of a brave young hunter. To avenge her death, he climbed up to the thunderbird nest with his war bow and arrows. The man killed the young eagles in the nest, then hid nearby to await the return of the parents. When they came back to the nest, the man let loose with his bow and pierced the giant birds with arrows. The injured birds were still able to fly and took to the air heading north. They never returned.

Nelson added a footnote to the story stating *"the truth of the tale is implicitly believed by the Eskimo of the lower Yukon. They point out the crater of an old volcano as the nest of the giant eagles and say that the ribs of old canoes and curiously colored stones carried there by the bird may still be seen about the rim of the nest. This is one of the various legends of the giant eagles or thunderbirds that are familiar to the Eskimo of the Yukon and to those of the Bering Strait and Kotzebue Sound."*

Nelson also collected thunderbird tales from the Diomede Islands in the Bering Strait where he found carved images of thunderbirds.

A member of the Haida nation told me about their thunderbird traditions. According to the Haida, the creature symbolizes supernatural power and is "the dominate force behind all of nature's doings." Only the most powerful leaders were allowed to have the thunderbird as a symbol.

A story related in *Princess Island Legends* tells of a young boy who was at the ocean's shore watching a pod of Sperm whales. As he watched the whales playing in the water, a terrible rumbling sound echoed from behind the mountains. As the boy listened, the sound grew louder, and he determined it was the clap of thunder rolling in. He turned his attention back to the whales, but moments later, he's startled by something unusual:

"A massive shadow spread across the water falling next to the boy. At first, he thought the shadow was from a cloud, but he changed his mind when he heard a horrendously loud screech from the sky. Looking up, he saw a giant bird swooping towards the ocean."

According to the tale, the bird's eyes *"flashed like lightning bolts,"* and the sound of thunder was produced by its wings. Claws opened wide, the bird dove towards the water.

"With a huge splash like geyser spray, the bird hit the water. The boy let out a terrorizing scream when he saw what was in the birds' talons. The bird, paying no attention to him, slowly rose from the water. Its powerful wings struggled to hold onto its prey. Water flowed from the Sperm whale as it struggled to free itself from the tight grip of the talons."

The young boy rushed home and told his grandfather what he had seen. The old man told the boy that he had witnessed the *"mighty thunderbird,"* a creature that the old man had seen himself in his youth.

While such tales can be viewed as mythical part and parcel of cultural traditions, it's important to note these aerial giants haven't been relegated to only legend and folklore. Modern sightings of giant birds in Alaska have cropped up over the years and continue to do so periodically.

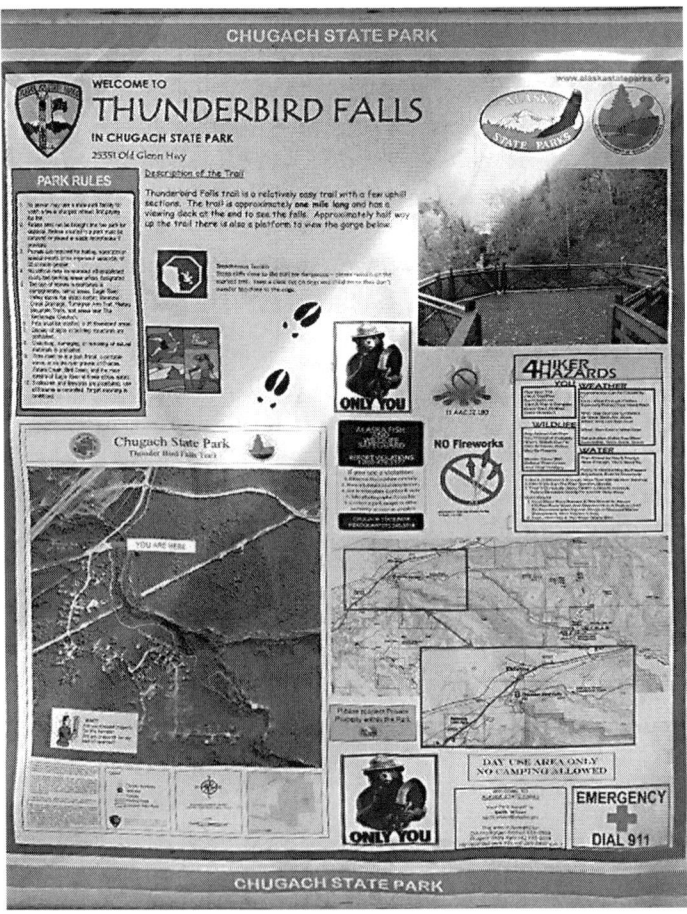

Thunderbird Falls, named after one of Alaska's cryptids

Modern Accounts

According to *Alaska Magazine,* there were reports of giant birds from towns near Kotzebue Sound in 1970 and 1972. The giants reportedly lived on nearby mountains. Mrs. Evelyn Barr of Noorvik, reported spotting a bird that looked bigger than a Twin Otter airplane. The Otter Floatplane De Haviland has a wingspan of 58 feet (17.7m). Mrs. Barr and her husband thought the bird was hunting caribou.

I found another listing for a 1970 giant bird sighting out of Selawik, north of Kivalina, though no details were listed.

A man in Anchorage told me he and his wife had seen a giant bird "as large as a small plane" in the mid-1980s. The sighting occurred while the couple were flying over Lake Iliamna. The bird was circling as if it was hunting prey.

2002 brought a series of sightings to the villages of Togiak and Manokotak. Forty-three-year-old Moses Coupchiak was working outside on October 10th when he saw a large object in the sky he thought was an airplane. As the object flew towards him, he realized it wasn't a plane but a living creature, a bird larger than any he'd ever seen before.

"'At first I thought it was one of those old-time Otter planes, instead of continuing toward me, it banked to the left, and that's when I noticed it wasn't a plane.'

The bird was 'something huge,' he said. 'The wing looks a little wider than the Otter's, maybe as long as the Otter plane.'"

Coupchiak said the bird flew behind a hill and disappeared. He rushed to his radio to warn people about the giant, airborne predator, telling them to get their children inside where they would be safe.

Sightings of the massive bird caught the attention of the *Anchorage Daily News.* The paper reported on the story in their October 18th edition. According to the story, witnesses were seeing "something out of Jurassic Park," flying in the region. The paper also recounted the testimony of John Bouker, a pilot who spotted the giant bird.

"A pilot says he spotted the creature while flying passengers to

173

Manokotak last week. He calculated that its wingspan matched the length of a wing on his Cessna 207. That's about 14 feet (4.3m).

Other people have put the wingspan in a similar range.

Scientists aren't sure what to make of the reports. No one doubts that people in the region west of Dillingham have seen a very large raptor-like bird. But biologists and other people familiar with big Alaska birds say they're skeptical it's that big."

John Bouker told the paper he'd been "highly skeptical" of accounts of giant birds and never put much thought into the possibility, at least, not until his own encounter. The *Daily News* described the incident:

"...early this week while flying into Manokotak, Bouker, owner of Bristol Bay Air Service, looked out his left window and 1,000 feet away, 'there's this big...bird,' he said.

'The people in the plane all saw him,' Bouker said. 'He's huge, he's huge, he's really, really big. You wouldn't want to have your children out.'

Nicolai Alakayak, a freight and passenger driver from Manokotak who was flying with Bouker, said the creature looked like an eagle and was as large as 'a little Super Cub.'"

As expected, scientists were quick to deny the possibility of birds the size of Super Cub planes.

"I'm certainly not aware of anything with a 14-foot (4.3m) wingspan that's been alive for the last 100,000 years," said federal raptor specialist Phil Schemf in Juneau.

Schemf, other biologists, a village police officer and teachers at the Manokotak School said sightings could be of a Steller's sea eagle, a species native to northeast Asia and one of the world's largest eagles. It's about 50 percent bigger than a bald eagle."

Skeptics were of course anxious to put down the notion that a giant bird was soaring in Alaskan skies. They quickly suggested that witnesses were probably seeing a Steller's sea eagle or some other large bird and mistaking the size.

Still, the story was big news, picked up by both Reuters and CNN.

Typically, it is difficult to judge the size of airborne objects, especially when there are no nearby objects to compare it with. Trained observers and pilots are of course in a different category since they are used to observing other objects when they are flying, and are typically more adept at judging air distance.

But not all scientists were quick to put down the reports. Federal biologist Karen Laing found the reports interesting and at least gave the locals some credit, stating:

"People don't always have the sizes right, but this is very different because the people in that area know what eagles look like. I don't know of any bird that's three times the size of an eagle. What would that be? What bird occurs here that would possibly be three times the size of an eagle or the size of a Super Cub?"

My friend and colleague, Ken Gerhard, has collected accounts of thunderbirds for years and has himself spent time in Alaska researching the topic. He relates an account he received from a man named David in 2011:

"I took my two sons last spring to a place called Tangle Lakes to fish for lake trout and camp out. The lakes are in open tundra mountains. Not many trees around the area. We decided to check one of the other lakes nearby. When we got to the lake we all saw a large bird that looked like a plane. It was so big. It swooped down to the middle of the lake and grabbed a big fish, then flew to the other side of the lake and landed. I jumped in my truck, drove around to the other side of the lake and watched him with binoculars. It ripped the fish to pieces and ate it. My boys and I never forgot that. It was amazing."

Gerhard relates another account, this one from a woman named Margaret who resides in the town of Nenana. Margaret's husband had worked in Denali National Park during the summer months of 2004-2005. An avid outdoorsman and hunter, the man told his wife about a giant bird he sighted:

"He told me he sighted a very large bird perched upon the rocky crags where he often stopped to look for mountain goats. Being familiar with this particular site, he had a good concept of distance and size; at first, he thought it was a human standing on the crags. He dragged out his binoculars and said he was shocked to see it was a bird, a very large bird. His estimate was a minimum of five feet (1.5m)

from head to tail. He stated that it was dark brown in color, mottled to lighter, somewhat like a juvenile golden eagle but much larger than any eagle he'd ever seen. The bird had its back to him. When it flew, it just dropped over the other side of the crags, so he only got a short glimpse of the wingspan, which he said was huge...again, larger than any eagle he'd ever seen."

Reportedly, other workers in Denali Park have also seen giant birds in the area.

Giant birds hit the news again in January 2018. This time the creature was flying over the Mendenhall Valley area of Juneau.

The reporting witness, Tabitha Bauer, posted her account online at the Juneau Community Collective, a Facebook group for locals to share news and information.

According to Bauer, she spotted the bird around 4 p.m. on January 16th. As she reported on the site:

"...I was just driving by the movie theatre in the Valley and there was a huge black bird flying above the road. The wingspan had to be at least 20 feet (6.1m). It was almost as wide as the road. I have lived here all my life and have never seen anything like that, it freaked me out. It was not a raven or an eagle. This isn't a joke. This thing was HUGE, almost the size of a small airplane. Did anyone else see it?"

The postings caught the attention of a local newspaper, *The Juneau Empire*, and reporters interviewed Bauer. Describing the bird to the paper, the woman said it was *"like an eagle but five times as big."*

The *Empire* also got some other details about the sighting from the witness. She said she was driving to the bank and was alone in her car at the time of the sighting. It was raining and she turned on her windshield wipers to clear her view. It was then that she spotted the jet-black bird. It was flying level with the treetops over Mendenhall Loop Road and coming towards her. The bird's tail was short, and Bauer said the creature flapped its wings, soared a bit higher and then flew at a fast pace over her car around fifty feet in the air. As she told the paper:

"I slowed down to try to get a better look at it. It was heading

toward the glacier; the wingspan was almost as wide as the road. It was the biggest thing I've ever seen in my life. It was very concerning. I've never seen anything like that."

Bauer reported she could not make out a beak but did notice feathers. She said the bird's body *"...had to have been six to eight feet. (1.8 – 2.4m)"*

The *Empire* also located another giant bird witness in the region. She recounted her story under the condition the paper only use her first name. "Diane" said she'd seen a giant bird perched, or attempting to perch, in a tree near her home at Lemon Creek several years previously.

Diane told the paper she stepped outside one night and discovered the birds in the area were in a very excited state.

"All you heard was the whooshing sound in my tree. I went inside and grabbed a flashlight. It was so large; I couldn't even get an outline of what type of bird it was.

That sounds crazy, but it was huge. I don't even go camping anymore."

Theories

Most traditional scientists quickly dismiss the notion of giant birds, pointing out that the witnesses "must" be mistaken in their estimate of the size of the animals they spot.

Cryptozoologists take a different approach by looking at possible explanations that are outside the box. Rare and reportedly extinct species are considered, as well as undiscovered animals.

Some researchers believe accounts of thunderbirds can be explained by sightings of the California condor. The carrion-eating bird once dominated the skies of the West and ranged from Baja, California up to the west coast of British Columbia.

As the largest land bird in North America with a wingspan of nearly ten feet (3m), the condor certainly would be an unusual sight, but the bird was almost extinct by the 19th century. Conservation efforts were launched in the 1980s and the bird was reintroduced to the California wilderness. The limited number of California condors makes it an unlikely candidate for modern Alaskan sightings, unless a population of them has survived hidden away in the state.

One bird that is often pointed to as an explanation for large bird sightings in the region is the Steller's sea eagle. The bird is native to Northeastern Asia and at times is found in areas of Alaska. The *Anchorage Daily News* noted that the Steller's sea eagle is about 50 percent larger than an American bald eagle and is one of the heaviest birds of prey known to exist. While not quite as large as the California condor, the bird does have a big wingspan, averaging between six and eight feet (1.8 – 2.4m). The uncommon bird may startle some observers who overestimate its overall wingspan.

Is it possible that an unknown species of giant bird still lives in remote regions of Alaska?

It's often presumed large species such as a thunderbird would be seen on a more regular basis if they existed, but large portions of Alaska are remote, and with the state's low population density, if the creature is to be found anywhere, the last frontier is certainly a prime location.

Living Mammoths

Often, cryptids are often animals that have never been scientifically proven to exist like bigfoot or the Mothman, but another type of animal also falls into the category; animals that once lived, are believed to be long extinct, yet are still spotted in modern times.

Examples of this type of cryptid include Australia's thylacine, or Tasmanian tiger. Declared officially extinct in 1936, sightings of the animal continue today.

An animal that vanished less than 100 years ago is one thing, but what about prehistoric creatures that have been gone for thousands of years? It's a question that arose in the 1800s when news circulated that mammoths were still surviving in arctic regions of the world.

First, a few points of clarity.

Mammoths were primitive elephants whose range spanned vast regions of Northern Asia, the Americas and Europe.

In early news accounts, reporters frequently used the terms mammoth and mastodon interchangeably, but this isn't scientifically correct. While they have a lot in common, mammoths and mastodons are two distinct species. According to Ross MacPhee, Ph.D., curator of the American Museum of Natural History in New York, mammoths arose around 5.1 million years ago in Africa. From there, they migrated throughout what is now Europe and North America.

It's commonly accepted that mammoths went extinct about 10,000 years ago, however, some scientists believe an isolated population of dwarf mammoths continued to thrive on Wrangle Island until about 3,700 years ago.

Mastodons came into existence much earlier, between 25-

30 million years ago. They lived mainly in North and Central America. They too went extinct around 10,000 years ago.

Both mammoths and mastodons were herbivores. Of the two, mammoths were slightly larger, but both species stood between seven and fourteen feet (2.1 -4.3m) in height. They were covered in long, shaggy hair that helped protect them from harsh conditions. The most well-known species of the mammoth is the wooly mammoth, noted for its coat of long, shaggy hair and massive curving tusks, long a staple of early depictions of prehistoric life.

Scientists generally believe the mammoth died out gradually from a combination of influences including the shrinking of their natural habitats. Some scientists believe early humans hunted mammoths and mastodons, further accelerating the extinction of the animals.

Frozen remains of wooly mammoths have been found in Alaska and Siberia giving scientists more information about the creatures than they have on most other prehistoric animals.

Tales from the 1800s claimed the animals were so well preserved that the meat was sliced off and fed to sled dog teams.

But beyond the frozen specimens, there were accounts from native Alaskans about the massive creatures roaming the vast tundra alive and well.

In 1891, native residents of the Yukon Territory reported seeing mammoths in the upper Stikine River area. The Copper River people of Interior Alaska described encounters with "huge, woolly beasts with horns like the trunks of birch trees," and said that in the winter, "puffs of steam issued from their nostrils like the escape pipe of a steamboat."

As explorers and miners began to trek though the frigid land, accounts of the creatures began to appear in newspapers. A news item from December 31, 1892 posted in the *Lawrence Daily Gazette* out of Lawrence, Kansas assumes people are already aware of living mastodons in Alaska. As the short news item reports:

"The well authenticated fact that a living mastodon has been

seen in the center of Alaska will fire Prof. Dyche's ambition like vitriol. The possession of a stuffed mammoth by the University would place it out of sight ahead of all the institutions on the continent. But how to find the game, how to kill it when found, how to bring the hide away when killed, and where to put it when mounted—these questions are calculated to abate the natural ardor the story of the discovery inspired."

A few years later, 1896, *The Portland Press* out of Portland, Maine ran a story about one Col. C. F. Fowler who worked for the Alaskan Fur and Commercial Company. The November 28th article reports that during one of his expeditions, Fowler was trading with local native Alaskan tribes who produced unusual ivory tusks. The men told Fowler the pieces were from a recent hunt. Intrigued by the out-of-place tusks, Fowler asked the men what animal they came from. The hunters described a beast that matched the supposedly long extinct mastodon.

Col. Fowler lived in Alaska from 1877-1889, a period of 12 years. He later told a reporter about his discovery of evidence of mammoths:

"Two years ago last summer I left Kodiak for a trip to the head waters of the Snake River, where our traveling agents had established a trading station at an Inuit village. The chief of this family of Inuit was named To-lee-ti-ma, and to him I was well recommended. He received me hospitably, and I at once began negotiations for the purchase of a big lot of fossil ivory which his tribe had stored near the village. The lot weighed several thousand pounds and was composed of the principal and inferior tusks of the mammoth, the remains of thousands of which gigantic animals are to be found in the beds of interior Alaskan water courses. I subjected the ivory to a rigid inspection, and upon two of the largest tusks I discovered fresh blood traces and the remnants of partly decomposed flesh. I questioned To-lee-ti-ma, and he assured me that less than three months before a party of his young men had encountered a drove of monsters about fifty miles above where he was then encamped, and had succeeded in killing two, an old bull and a cow. At my request he sent for the leader of the hunting party, a young and very intelligent Indian, and I questioned him closely about his adventure among a race of animals that the scientific people claim are extinct. He told a very straightforward story and I have no reason to

doubt its truth.

He and his band were searching along a dry water course for ivory and had found a considerable quantity. One of the party, who was in advance, rushed in upon the main body one morning with the startling intelligence that at a spring of water about a mile above where they then were he had discovered the 'sign' of several of the 'big-teeth.' They had come to the spring to drink from a lofty plateau further inland and had evidently fed in the vicinity of the water for some time. The chief immediately called about him his warriors, and the party, under the leadership of the scout, approached the stream. They had nearly reached it when their ears were suddenly saluted by a chorus of loud, shrill, trumpet-like calls, and an enormous creature came crashing toward them through the thicket, the ground fairly trembling with its ponderous footfalls. With wild cries of terror and dismay the Indians fled, all but the chief and the scout who had first discovered the trail of the monster. They were armed with large caliber muskets and stood their ground, opening fire on the mammoth. A bullet must have penetrated the creature's brain, for it staggered forward and fell dead and subsequently on their way back to their campground they overhauled and killed a cow 'big-teeth,' which was evidently the mate of the first one killed. I asked the hunter to describe the monster and taking a sharp stick he drew me a picture of the pale animal in the soft clay. According to his description it was at least twenty feet (6.1m) in height and thirty feet (9.1m) in length. In general shape it was not unlike an elephant, but its ears were smaller, its eyes bigger and its trunk longer and more slender. Its tusks were yellowish-white in color and six in number. Four of these tusks were placed like those of a boar, one on either side in each jaw; they were about four feet (1.2m) long and came to a sharp point. The other two tusks he brought away. 'I measured them, and they were over fifteen feet (4.6m) in length and weighed upward of 250 pounds (113kg) each. They gradually tapered to a sharp point and curved inward. The monster's body was covered with long, coarse hair of a reddish dun color.'"

A British correspondent for the journal *Science Gossip* was quite enthusiastic about the news of living mammoths and believed the creatures would soon be on display for all to see. He wrote with much zeal in the journal:

"Upon the whole there seems a very good chance that we may yet

see a living mammoth in the Zoological Gardens in Regent's Park, and that we may have the pleasure of feeding it with buns."

Obviously, the animals never made it to any zoological displays in Europe.

In 1893, the *Winnipeg Daily Free Press* of Winnipeg, Manitoba reported that Alaskans were seeing mammoths "running about." The paper's March 28th edition reported:

"The Stickeen Indian positively assert that within the last five years they have frequently seen animals which, from the descriptions given, must have been mastodons.

Last spring, while out hunting, one of the Indians came across a series of large tracks, each the size of the bottom of a salt barrel, sunk deep in the moss. He followed the curious trail for some miles, finally coming out in full view of his game says The Philadelphia Ledger.

As a class these Indians are the bravest of hunters, but the proportions of this new spectacle of game filled the hunter with terror, and he took to swift and immediate flight. He described the creature as being as large as a post trader's store, with great, shining, yellowish white tusks, and a mouth large enough to swallow a man with one gulp. He further says that the animal was undoubtedly of the same species as those whose bones and tusks lie all over that section of the country.

The fact that other hunters have told of seeing these monsters browsing on the herbs up along the river gives a certain probability to the story. Over on Forty Mile Creek, bones of mastodons are quite plentiful. One ivory tusk, nine feet (2.7m) long, projects from one of the sand dunes on that creek, and single teeth have been found so large that they would be a good load for one man to carry. I believe that the mule-footed hog still exists; also, that live mastodons play tag with the aurora every night over on Forty Mile Creek in Alaska."

In 1896, a story out of Juneau reported that mastodons could still be found in the wilds of Alaska and that native hunters were reporting encounters with them. For the most part, the story rehashed the 1893 accounts. The 1896 report made the rounds, being published in newspapers all over the country under the headline "Living Mastodons." The news furthered the idea that living mammoths were roaming the Alaskan countryside.

185

The '96 news accounts also included a colorful description of the beast from a native man as well as commentary about the location where the creatures were to be found:

"He described it as being larger than Harper's (the post trader's store), with great shining yellow tusks, and a mouth large enough to swallow him at a single gulp. He said the animal was undoubtedly the same as were the huge bones scattered over that section.

If such an animal is now in existence and there is no doubt as to the veracity of the Indian, as other Indians as well as Mr. Harper, had confirmed it, they inhabit a section of very high altitude, and one but rarely visited by human beings and those only Indians. We have no reason to doubt the Indians tale for at no very distant period the Yukon country was inhabited by these animals, and hundreds of their massive skeletons found strewn along the creeks are the silent but 'truthful witnesses.'"

Some researchers believe tales of surviving mammoths came from discoveries of frozen specimens. It's clear large numbers of remains were being found as more explorers trekked across the frozen landscape. In some cases, the remains were so well preserved it gave the impression the animals had been alive and well days before.

An article from the *Alaska Searchlight* in its February 12, 1898 edition includes a report from a well-known missionary Reverend Sheldon Jackson, Jackson was the founder of Sheldon Jackson College in Sitka and spent many years in the region. Jackson reports the discovery of frozen mammoths at a location in Interior Alaska. As the *Searchlight* reported:

"Five years ago, I started on a journey from our mission house on the lower Yukon, intending to be absent five months, visiting all the missionary stations under the Arctic Circle. I was accompanied on this journey by three Eskimos and six of the best dogs in the mission, harnessed to sleds...We had traveled 2,000 miles (3,219km) northeasterly, making our last stopping place Kazatka Lake, a body of water thirty miles (48km) long and twenty miles (32km) wide, with rugged mountains on either side, and a flat and marshy valley at either end, with a river flowing out from the south. At the intersection of mountain and river there were glaciers common to the whole country,

but these possessed peculiarities that alone belonged to them. They were dead glaciers, by reason of having lost their means of locomotion.

There is nothing as noisy as a live, moving glacier—nothing so dead and silent as the glacier that has lost its legs. But there were legs imbedded in the ice; they were there by the hundreds and I may truly say by the thousands and were attached to huge animals, the mastodons or "elephants of the arctic," on their haunches, with large trunks hanging between massive ivory tusks. They were caught in the embrace of the deadly foe, which preserved them as freshly as though they had been imprisoned but yesterday.

Taking a knife from my belt, I slashed a piece of meat and gave it to the dogs, and they ate it as ravenously as though sliced from a quarter of a moose."

As the turn of the century neared, people were still excited about the prospect of surviving mammoths.

Alfred P. Swineford, Governor of Alaska from 1885-1889 reportedly commented on the animals stating:

"There are mastodons on several high plateaus of the Alaskan interior."

In 1899, a man named Henry Tukeman claimed he'd killed a mammoth and donated the body to the Smithsonian Institution in Washington, D.C. In short order, the story was proven to be false.

The *Evening Messenger* out of Marshall, Texas ran a story about "Alaska's Living Mastodons" in its September 5, 1899 edition. The story read in part:

"The Land of Wonders Lays Another Claim to Distinction"

"The remarkable assertion is made by a member of the Alaska Historical Society, writing in the Forest and Stream, that perhaps the mastodons, remains of which have been found in a well-preserved condition in various parts of Alaska and Siberia, are not yet entirely extinct, as has hitherto been believed, but that almost conclusive evidence to the contrary has been recently brought to light.

It has been a well-known fact that the Eskimos have traded in the tusks and bones of this animal for centuries, and great deposits of them have been found, while arctic explorers have even fed their dogs on their carcasses preserved in the ice, supposedly from pre-historic times. The district reported to be thus inhabited is very high and well supplied with moss, grass and fodder in unlimited quantities, as well as plenty of water, and consequently it is argued that whatever natural force may have destroyed and buried the immense numbers who remains are found in great masses in this particular section was probably free from its effects which accounts for the existence of a remnant of the race."

Reports dropped off dramatically in the early 1900s. Reportedly Dr. J.P. Frizzel discovered "fresh" tracks on Unimak Island in the Aleutian chain in 1903. According to the September 29th edition of the *Nome Semi-Weekly News*:

"I do not wish to make myself ridiculous to the scientific world by stating as a fact that at least one living specimen of the mammoth family is still roaming at large on the American side in the far arctic regions. However, I saw, with my own eyes, comparatively fresh tracks that apparently could not have been made by any other kind of animal but a mammoth. I ran across the animal's tracks on the Island of Unimak, which is 125 miles (201km) around and twenty-six miles (42km) in width. It is about four miles (6km) from the mainland, and animals can walk back and forth from the Island.

The tracks could be distinctly seen in the ice and snow, and I followed them for quite a distance. They sank four inches (10cm) into the hard, frozen ground. They were four feet (1.2m) apart, showing that distance to be the stride of the animal. The width of the tracks was nineteen by twenty inches (48 x 51cm). In each track was the distinct impression of eighteen toes."

From my friend and colleague Nick Redfern comes a very strange Alaskan mammoth sighting. Nick interviewed a woman named Jill O'Brien who claimed she saw a baby mammoth in Alaska in September 2008. Well, sort of.

The encounter took place in Wrangell-St. Elias National Park and Preserve. Established in 1980 by Alaska's National Interest Lands Conservation Act, the park covers an area in excess of thirteen million acres, (13.2 million acres (5.3 million hectares) to be exact), making it the largest National Park in the United States.

In a tale that takes a big turn from the idea of a surviving, physical mammoth, O'Brien believes she saw something quite unusual.

The woman was at the base of Mount St. Elias, a mountain that rises to over 18,000 feet (5,486m). As she was taking photos of the vast scenery, she heard what she described to Redfern as a *"thudding and crunching on the ground"* behind her.

Turning around, fearful that she was about to meet one of Alaska's large bears, Jill received a shock. As Nick writes:

"Jill found herself confronted by a very small mammoth, one that was somewhere in the region of four feet (4.2m) *in height, or maybe slightly bigger."*

As the woman watched the creature approach, she received a further surprise with what happened next:

"As Jill watched in a mixture of awe and shock, the mini-mammoth raced past her and...vanished. Gone. When I asked Jill to explain what she meant, she said that the animal was suddenly enveloped by a small 'black cloud,' which 'sucked into itself' and disappeared. The entire encounter lasted barely a handful of seconds at most. Jill was, however, very sure of what she had seen."

It's difficult to say exactly what Jill O'Brien experienced. Clearly animals, even prehistoric ones, have never been known to vanish in black clouds.

O'Brien herself suggested an explanation; she believes she saw the ghost of a mammoth.

Redfern himself admits it's an odd case, one sure to ruffle the feathers of many cryptozoologists who hold to the flesh and bone reality of cryptid sightings and encounters. He writes:

"Whether Jill's case is one for ghost-hunters, or for cryptozoologists, is something well worth pondering on."

Indeed, such accounts usually create far more questions than they answer and fling the door further open in terms of exactly what else could explain cryptid sightings.

In recent years, a number of "mammoth" videos have

surfaced online. Purporting to be modern footage of surviving wooly mammoths, the videos are clearly hoaxed, often poorly, leaving us with no convincing evidence that any species of mammoth still survives.

Legendary cryptozoologist Bernard Heuvelmans mentioned the idea of surviving mammoths in his book *On the Track of Unknown Animals*, noting a reported story from Siberia dated 1918 that involved a hunter tracking a mammoth for several days. Reportedly, Siberian tribespeople have stories of surviving mammoths out on the frozen tundra in their land. They described the creatures as "large shaggy beasts."

Like other researchers, Heuvelmans suggested the possibility that mammoths lived longer than is commonly accepted. If this is true, tribal cultures likely have tales passed down in their oral traditions that involve hunts of the animal.

Thanks to modern science, tales of mammoths might not stay in the past. As much as it sounds like a plot line from Jurassic Park, scientists are seriously looking at the idea of bringing mammoths back.

The existence of frozen soft tissue remains and DNA from wooly mammoths has led experts to believe the species could be brought back by scientific means. The mammoth genome project was completed in 2015, and since then, several methods for reviving the animals have been proposed.

As the modern science of cloning continues to develop, one of the test subjects that scientists are putting the most attention on is the mammoth. Researchers at several locations, including Harvard, are currently considering the process.

One suggested method involves the artificial insemination of an elephant egg cell with sperm cells from a frozen wooly mammoth. The resulting calf would be an elephant-mammoth hybrid. After several repetitions of this process, an almost pure wooly mammoth would be produced.

Another commonly discussed process would utilize the DNA of mammoths and the egg cell of a female elephant. The process, called somatic cell nuclear transfer, would involve the divided cell being implanted in a living female elephant. The resulting calf would have the genes of the wooly mammoth.

While still in development, it may not be long before scientists take serious steps to bringing back this lost species.

For some, it's a romantic notion, the concept that a species somehow continued despite all odds and outward appearances, but all things considered, it's highly unlikely that mammoths continue to thrive in the Alaskan wilderness.

Still, one never knows what could be wandering on the remote Arctic Tundra, and with the cloning project currently underway, some of us may live to hear the thundering footsteps of mammoths!

Alaska has an abundance of bears

A Land of Bears

Alaska is a land of bears. All three species of North American bears flourish in the state: polar bears, black bears, and brown bears (which includes grizzlies). Residents and visitors alike see bears frequently; fortunately, sightings are usually from a safe distance.

State wildlife officials emphasize that even if you don't see a bear, you're never far from one, and they stress the importance of safety whenever any species of bear is nearby. They may look cute and cuddly to some, but they are extremely dangerous animals. Encounters with aggressive bears are rare but wise locals take common sense precautions to deter the animals from coming near their homes.

With so many bears present in the region, it's no surprise they play a big part in native Alaskan legends and lore.

Qoqogaq

The Inuit describe a huge, white bear they call the *Qoqogaq*. Stories of the creature have been passed down through the tribe's traditions for ages. It's described as a massive beast with a head five feet (1.5m) wide and ten powerful legs. The ten-legged beast is said to live in the Northwestern region of Alaska, between Point Barrow and Cape Prince of Wales.

One report of a *Qoqogaq* encounter comes from 1913. A group of Inuit hunters were trekking east from Point Barrow when they heard something very large moving around below them under the thick layer of ice. One of the hunters inadvertently made a loud sound which caught the creature's attention. Its massive head suddenly burst through the ice and the creature came towards the men. Only good fortune and fast sled dogs saved the group from the jaws of the massive animal.

Aside from scant, brief stories, tales of the ten-legged bear are difficult to find. One account can be found in *The Alaskan Ten Footed Bear and Other Legends*. Despite the title, the small pamphlet only contains one reference to the creature, a very short account related by an Eskimo man named Tarah who said his grandfather had encountered the ten-footed bear. Tarah says the bear lives most of its time in the water like a seal:

"But he is very big, and his fur is long and white. His nose is black on the end, and his ears are small and lie flat against his head."

Tarah goes on to explain that the bear looks like a polar bear, but has ten feet, five on each side of its body.

Whether the ten-footed bear is a lost cryptid or simply something from tribal folklore, there are certainly other reports of unusual bears in Alaska.

The Short-Faced Bear

Modern science says the North American short-faced bear went extinct about 11,000 years ago. The apex predator lived during a time when dire wolves and saber-toothed cats roamed the continent. But the short-faced bear was likely at the top of the food chain.

On all fours, the short-faced bear would have been eye to eye with a grown man, five to six feet (1.5 – 1.8m) in height. Standing on its hind legs, it would have been a staggering ten to twelve feet (3 – 3.7m) tall. The short-faced bear was not only large, it was also fast. With longer legs than modern bears, it's speculated the animal could obtain speeds of up to 40 miles per hour (64km/h), though it may have been even faster. By contrast, grizzly bears can reach speeds up to 35 miles an hour (56km/h) and reach an average height of 6 - 7 feet (1.8 – 2.1m).

The short-faced bear also had distinctive feet, with toes that face forward rather than inward, as in other bears.

Paul Matheus, former Director of the Alaska Quaternary Center, has done extensive research on *Arctodus*, or the short-face bear. He believes the animals weighed between 1,600 to 1,900 pounds (726 – 862kg), roughly twice the weight of the average Alaskan coastal brown bear.

A 1967 paper by University of Helsinki's Dr. Bjorn Kurten brought the ancient predator to the attention of scholars. Kurten said *Arctodus* was *"…by far the most powerful predator in the Pleistocene fauna of North America."*

As impossible as it sounds, some believe the creature still exists in remote regions of Alaska.

Reports have surfaced over the years of unusually large bears in Arctic regions. Many of the reports are likely explainable by sightings of large specimens of polar bears, but at times, the witnesses describe unusual features, particularly a "short face" and large head. Such descriptions indicate they may have spotted something more unusual than a large member of a known species.

American explorer, author and outdoorsman Caspar Whitney described his sighting of an unusual bear:

"It is a peculiar looking bear, seeming a cross between the grizzly and the polar, and it has this peculiarity, that its hind claws are as big as the fore claws, while its head looks somewhat like that of an Eskimo dog, very broad in the forehead, with square, long muzzle, and ears set on quite like the dog's. It is very wide at the shoulders, and its robe in color resembles the grizzly."

While not an Alaskan report, one historical note that does bear mentioning comes from the Kamchatka Peninsula of Russia. Much like Alaska, the Kamchatka Peninsula is a region with a low human population and plenty of rugged, untouched territory.

In 1920, zoologist Sten Bergman examined a pelt that he believed came from a subspecies of brown bear. Bergman also noted larger than normal bear tracks in the region. Legends from the area spoke of a creature known as the "God Bear," a massive beast with a unique appearance.

Another Alaskan story claims that in 1972, a young man set out into the wild outside the village of Yakutat. His stated goal was to "commune with bears," probably not the wisest decision in the wilds of Alaska.

Reportedly, the man disappeared in the Wrangle Mountains

but was found months later near an inlet at Icy Bay. The man was alive but had been severely mauled. He died of his wounds, but before doing so, rambled about "giant bears with short snouts."

Whether the story is fact or folklore is unknown. To date, I've had no luck tracking down any news sources or witnesses to the incident.

It's easy to think that people reporting a relic ancient creature are simply mistaking a known animal for something unusual, but some accounts are harder to accept as simply a case of mistaken identity.

My late colleague J.C. Johnson related an account to me involving a hunter in Alaska who was positive he'd spotted a short-faced bear in the late 1990s. The man was a seasoned hunter and had encountered many "normal" bears in the wild. He later did his own research to find out what kind of bear he'd seen and came upon an artistic depiction of the short-faced bear. *"Without a doubt,"* he told Johnson, *"that's what I saw on the Alaskan Tundra. I've hunted bears and I've spent a good portion of my life going to remote parts of Alaska. I can ID any type of known bear. This thing was not a normal known species."*

Whether or not prehistoric bears have somehow survived in Alaska is still unknown but what is certain is that hybrid bears have been found in the state and they may explain many of the unusual sightings.

Hybrids

Sometimes known as "grolar bears" or "pizzly bears," hybrid bears have been confirmed both in captivity and in the wild in Alaska as well as other Arctic regions.

In 1864, naturalist Roderick MacFarlane was given an unusual bear hide and skull by Inuit hunters. MacFarlane was staying at Fort Anderson in Canada's Northwest Territories when he received the items. The hide had yellowish hair and the skull was misshapen with an odd tooth formation not like other, known bears of the time.

The Inuits told MacFarlane the hide came from one of the massive bears that roamed remote areas of their tribal lands.

MacFarlane sent the pieces to the Smithsonian Institute in Washington, D.C. The Smithsonian filed the hide and skull away in their archives where it remained until 1918 when zoologist Clinton Heart Merriam discovered it and examined it closely.

Merriam believed the hide was not a brown bear as initially suspected. He proposed the bear was a newly discovered species and dubbed it *"Vetularctos inopinatus,"* or, the Ancient Unexpected Bear.

Scientists were eventually able to determine that the creature was a grizzly/polar bear hybrid.

Grizzly bears are a subspecies of brown bear that tend to live and breed on land. Polar bears prefer the water and ice and usually breed on ice. Although the two species are genetically similar and often found in the same territory, they usually avoid each other in the wild since they tend towards different ecological niches.

Hybrids between the two possess a range of characteristics of both types of bears. Brown fur on the paws, long claws, and grizzly-like heads are common traits.

A study by biologists with the American Museum of Natural History documented evidence that grizzlies have been migrating into polar bear territory, a process that is creating further opportunities for hybrid bears to be born.

More Giants

First Nations peoples have long mentioned bears of massive size in the region, referring to them as "king bears," or "weasel bears."

In 2014, a giant bear skull was found on a beach in northern Alaska. Measuring just over 16 inches (41cm) from the tip of the nose to the back of the skull, experts described the skull as unusually slender and elongated in shape. Radiocarbon dating revealed the skull was about 1,300 years old. It was found at an archaeological site known as Walapka, a few miles from Utqiagvi (formerly known as Barrow) just after a storm.

"We don't know the exact size, but we do know it was a huge

bear," said Dr. Anne Jensen. "It is adult, and not a young one since all the cranial sutures—place where the skull plates join—are fused and can barely be seen."

Jensen noted that it wasn't only the size of the skull that made it unusual:

"The main thing is the differences in the skull morphology, the shape of the skull. The back of the skull is longer and comparatively narrow...with features that are noticeably different from those of modern polar bears. The front part of the skull, from roughly the eyes forward, is like that of typical polar bears."

Scientists nicknamed the skull "the Old One." Opinions on the creature's roots are varied, some believe it's a subspecies of polar bear rather than a separate species. When asked if bears the size of the Old One were still roaming Alaska, Jensen replied "Certainly."

God bears, giants and hybrids are all part of the lore of bears in Alaska and obviously the rugged landscape is still revealing secrets.

Out of Place Big Cats

Alaska certainly isn't a place you would expect to find exotic cats wandering around. There are tidbits here and there of sightings of prehistoric looking large cats, reported sabretooth tigers and other curious bits of lore. Unfortunately, the accounts are so slim in detail and often "friend of a friend" type tales that it's hard to know if there's any real substance to them, or if it's strictly folklore. Nevertheless, there are a couple of unusual sightings of big cats in the state that have been documented by news sources.

In 1956 the *Evening News* out of Port Angeles, Washington reported a strange big cat sighting in Alaska. According to a story by Charles J. Keim in the paper's July 10th edition, an Anchorage guide with over 25 years' experience recounted the tale of a bush pilot's sighting.

"He said that a bush pilot friend of his spotted a strange animal walking along the coast when he was on a flying trip. The pilot brought his plane lower and got a good view of the animal which appeared to be a tiger. He believed that it was a Siberian tiger that came to Alaska via the ice floes.

Otto [William Geist, University of Alaska paleontologist] said that could be possible, but the tiger would have had to have come from the Mongolian side where they live.

He added that there once were tigers in Alaska before the Pleistocene period (the glacial epoch or ice age 20-30,000 years ago). How does he know? He had retrieved their preserved bones from frozen muck in various areas in the territory."

Did an exotic tiger wander so far out of its natural territory? It's possible of course, but since there were no further accounts reported, it's difficult to determine what the truth of the sighting was.

Mountain lions don't normally call Alaska home, though occasional sightings crop up. A tourist reported seeing a mountain lion near Jean Lake in 1988, and in 1991, one was spotted in the Haines area.

A news item from more recent years involves sightings of African lions in Alaska. According to the *Daily News* out of Anchorage, five people spotted the cats in 1995. The July 27th edition of the paper reports:

"Cat's Out of the Bag on Kenai

Five People Tell Fish and Game They've Seen an African Lion

Four people reported seeing a maned lion along the Sterling Highway on the north side of Kenai Lake. It was about noon, and they saw it from about 100 yards (91m) *away.*

Ten days later, a man reported seeing a female African lion."

The last witness was 44-year-old Chris Winans who spotted the lion crossing Snug Harbor Road on the south side of Kenai Lake. Winans' told reporters:

"It really took my breath away. I saw the whole thing in clear profile for two or three seconds. My first reaction was that it looks like a female African lion. My next thought was that can't be up here. It's got to be a cougar or a lynx. But it was way too big."

Winans said the animal was bigger than a Great Dane with an S-shaped tail, powerful rear legs and a small, catlike head. Winans was positive he'd spotted a female lion, but earlier witnesses said the cat they'd seen was a male as they'd noticed its mane.

State wildlife officials took note of the reports and were on alert. Naturally, there was speculation that the cat was a mountain lion. Not completely impossible, but certainly not common. The only mountain lion ever confirmed in Alaska was killed in the town of Wrangell in 1989. Officials believed at the time the animal was an escaped pet, but it could have wandered down from the Stikine River and out of its normal range.

State wildlife officials speculated that lions or other big cats could be out there and may have been released into the wild:

"It could be somebody's pet who grew up on them. We deal a lot with animals released along the roadside by somebody who says, 'Here, now you're Born Free.' Though this would certainly be one of the more unusual cases."

Officials expressed a hope to live catch the lion, or lions, if the opportunity arose, alas, it never did, and no further reports of the rogue African cats surfaced in the area.

Dog Mushing, Alaska's state sport

Canine Legends

The Iditarod Trail sled dog race has been an annual event in Alaska since 1967. The race is held in early March on a course that runs from Anchorage to Nome. Portions of the trail were used by native Alaskans for hundreds of years before the arrival of Russian fur traders in the 1800s.

First Nations people in the region have varied views on dogs. The animals were useful for travel, but also good to have nearby since they were said to offer protection from certain supernatural creatures, namely the *Kushtaka*.

The Inuit have legends of a creature called the *Adlet*. The beast has the lower body of a dog and the upper body of a human being.

The *Adlet* is reportedly bloodthirsty and bears similarities to the European werewolf, attacking humans whenever the opportunity arose.

Another Inuit canid creature is the *Keelut*, a manifestation of an evil spirit in the form of a black dog. The *Keelut* is almost completely hairless, only having patches of hair on its feet.

It's said the *Keelut's* tracks vanish, making it impossible to follow. The creature prowls the night, stalking travelers and killing them.

Another canine creature people claim to have spotted in modern times is a beast known as the *Waheela*.

The Waheela

Inuit legend includes tales of a large, snow white wolf known as the *Waheela*.

The *Waheela* is larger than a normal wolf with a wide head

and proportionally larger feet. Tracks from the animal exhibit widely spaced toes. The waheela's fur is said to be snow white and long, and its hind legs shorter than its front legs.

Witnesses describe the creature as 3 ½ to 4 feet (1 – 1.2m) tall at the shoulder. They are solitary animals and never seen in packs. The creatures reportedly roam remote areas of the far north, preferring areas with little or no human population.

First Nations legends say the *Waheela* is an evil spirit with otherworldly powers and strange deaths have been attributed to the creature.

While wolves normally inhabit the Arctic regions of Alaska and Canada's Northwest Territories, they are of the normal variety.

Cryptozoologist Ivan Sanderson mentioned a large wolf account from Canada's Nahanni Valley that matched descriptions of the *Waheela*. Sanderson received the account from a man listed as "Frank," who told him the beast stood 3 ½ feet (1m) tall at the shoulder, had a broad head, short legs and a shaggy white coat.

Sanderson also mentioned that his friend, Tex Zeigler had reported sightings of the *Waheela* on the Alaskan Tundra.

Early European trappers working in Alaska also reported large wolves on occasion.

One man reported seeing an unusual wolf while he was out hunting in a remote, northern area of the state in the 1980s. The man said the wolf had a head several times larger than a normal wolf and stood almost four feet (1.2m) high at its shoulders.

Some people speculate the *Waheela* is a species of bear-dog that once lived in North America. As the name implies, bear-dogs looked like a hybrid between a bear and a dog. Although the animal did exist, it has been extinct for some five million years, so it's an unlikely explanation for what people have spotted in the wild north.

There could, however, be unusually large wolves living in remote areas of the state where they would not be seen frequently.

Volcanoes on the Kamchatka Peninsula.
Photo: Dr. Igor Smolyar, NODC, NOAA
Courtesy: National Oceanic and Atmospheric Administration

Steller's Amazing Animals

Georg Wilhelm Steller was a German zoologist, botanist, physician and explorer active in the 1700s. He's considered a pioneer of Alaskan natural history and chronicled many animals that now bear his name including the Steller's jay, Steller's sea eagle and Steller's sea lion.

In the mid-1700s, Steller took part in a major expedition to the arctic under the command of Captain Vitus Bering. The expedition crew was mainly German and Russian, except for the Captain who was of Danish origin.

Steller left St. Petersburg in 1738 and joined the expedition in the Spring of 1740, serving as scientist and physician. The Fall of 1740 found Steller sailing to the Kamchatka Peninsula with Bering's two ships, the St. Peter and the St. Paul.

Steller had volunteered for the position and hoped to document the natural world of the Russian Empire's eastern reaches. After spending the winter of 1740 on the east coast of Kamchatka, Bering summoned Steller to join the voyage in search of a passage to America. Steller crossed the peninsula by dog sled and joined Bering on board the St. Peter.

From there, the expedition was fraught with difficulties. Bering's two ships became separated in a storm and the St. Peter sailed east looking for land. Steller argued with Bering since his scientific data indicated they should sail northeast. After considerable time, the ship turned in Steller's suggested direction and finally found land.

Steller had to argue for time on land to document his findings. He was able to get ten hours to explore when the ship made landfall on Kayak Island in 1741. Steller is credited as being the first non-native person to set foot on Alaskan soil.

Between his challenges of getting time on land, and his disagreements with the Captain's sense of direction, there's speculation that Steller and Bering didn't get along well at all.

Despite the difficulties, Steller managed to chronicle a range of animals during his brief ten hours, and continued to collect information on the rest of the journey.

As the expedition continued, a scurvy epidemic broke out amongst the crew. Steller treated himself and his assistant with herbs and berries he gathered, but the ship's officers rejected his proposal to treat the crew with the same remedies. The epidemic was devasting and half of the crew died. By the time the expedition turned for home, only twelve men were able to work the rigging. Between the storms, arctic conditions, and insufficient crewmen, the St. Peter was in a battered condition. The vessel was shipwrecked on an island, a piece of land that became known as Bering Island.

Steller did his best to tend to the survivors. Captain Bering was unable to fight off the scurvy and died. Those who remained set up camp under harsh conditions. Aside from being sick, they had little food or water at hand. Arctic foxes started raiding the camp and the men had to fight them off. The men were stranded on the island for eight months. When weather conditions improved in early 1742, the remaining crew managed to salvage enough material from the St. Peter to construct another small vessel. They dubbed it *The Bering* and were able to make their way off the island.

During his time shipwrecked on Bering Island, Steller wrote *De Bestiis Marinis,* a detailed account of the animals he encountered and documented during the expedition.

Steller spent two more years exploring the Kamchatka peninsula before leaving to return to Russia. He died on the journey back in November 1746. His journals, notes and other documents were given to the Academy in St. Petersburg and were published posthumously.

Several of the animals Steller documented during his time in the region now have an air of mystery about them for various reasons. Some are of course well known to modern science, but others remain in the cryptid category.

Steller's Sea Ape

The oddest of Steller's animals is known as the sea ape.

Steller spotted the animal in the waters off Alaska's Shumagin Islands in 1741. It wasn't just a quick sighting. Steller wrote that he observed the animal for several hours.

He watched the beast raise its front end up out of the water and he believed the creature was observing the ship. As the naturalist watched, the animal engaged in a "juggling behavior" with a piece of seaweed.

Although a lot of varied animals had been seen on the journey, the creature was something new for Steller. As he recounts in his journal:

"During this time, we were near land or surrounded by it we saw large numbers of hair seals, sea otters, fur seals, sea lions, and porpoises..."

"On August 10, we saw a very unusual and unknown sea animal, of which I am going to give a brief account since I observed it for two whole hours. It was about two Russian ells [five feet] (1.5m) in length, the head was like a dog's, with pointed, erect ears. From the upper and lower lips on both sides, whiskers hung down...The eyes were large; the body was longish round and thick, tapering gradually towards the tail. The skin seemed thickly covered with hair, of a grey color on the back but reddish white on the belly; in the water, however, the animal appeared equally reddish and cow colored. The tail was divided into two fins, of which the upper, as in the case of sharks, was twice as large as the lower. Nothing struck me more surprising than the fact that neither forefeet as in the marine amphibians nor, in their stead, fins were to be seen."

Steller even tried to shoot the animal, firing off several shots, but he missed, and the creature swam away. Steller's account in his journal is the only entry he made regarding the animal. Leaving it a puzzle with very few pieces.

Some researchers believe Steller saw a known animal, such as a young, Northern fur seal and misidentified it. It's an argument that gives little credit to Steller's background and track record. The naturalist was already very familiar with fur seals and it's highly unlikely he would have mistaken one for the unusual creature he was describing.

Cryptozoologist Roy P. Mackal speculates that Steller had spotted a juvenile specimen of an unknown, long-necked pinniped.

Another possible explanation is that the explorer spotted a species that has since gone extinct.

Still other researchers have posited that the animal was a complete fabrication on Steller's part, a way to take a jab at Captain Bering whom he reportedly despised. Those who support this theory point to the fact that Steller named the creature *Simia marina Danica,* or, "Danish Sea Ape."

Obviously, we can't at this point know what Steller's sense of humor was like or exactly how aggravated he was with the captain. Those who refute this theory find it unlikely that such a serious man of the natural sciences would put such a thing in his journals and note that the rest of his writings are of a serious and scientific nature.

Intriguingly, the animal may have surfaced again in the late 1960s.

In his book, *Misty Islands,* sailor Miles Smeeton wrote about his encounter with an unusual animal in 1969.

Smeeton was sailing his vessel, the *Tzu Hang* in the Aleutian Islands. Sailing with him was his daughter Clio, and a friend named Henry. On the day of the sighting, the *Tzu Hang* was headed for a location called Deep Cove on the northern coast of Atka Island. Smeeton relates the incident:

"...on the way saw a strange animal. In all the thousands of miles that Tzu Hang has sailed we have seen nothing that could be described as mysterious or unaccountable, except this one beast that we all forgot about in the interest of arriving at Deep Cove.

Clio, Henry, and I were on deck when it occurred.

'Look, look,' cried Clio, suddenly pointing close off the weather bow. 'What is it, what is it?'

Close off the port bow an animal was lying in the water; it looked to be about the size of a sheep and had long, pepper-and-salt hair like a cairn terrier, of a reddish-yellow color. As the bow approached, it made a slow, undulating dive and disappeared beneath the ship. What most impressed me was the length of its hair, about four to five inches (10 – 13cm) long; and when I first saw it on the surface the hair was floating round the body like weed growing on a half-submerged rock. I never saw its head, but Clio, who also saw it come up on the other side of the ship and look at us, said that the head was more like the head of a dog than of a seal, with the eyes close together, not set on the side of the head like a seal's. Henry confirmed this impression, saying that it had a face like a Tibetan terrier, with drooping Chinese whiskers."

Much later, Smeeton doesn't specify how long, his daughter Clio was in South Africa and read a book called *Where the Sea Breaks its Back* by Corey Ford. In the book, Ford related the account of Steller's sea ape and reading the story reminded Clio of the incident aboard her father's vessel. As Smeeton recalls:

"...Clio remembered our own strange animal and wrote to remind me. Clio, Henry and I had all forgotten the sighting, but now we all believe that the animal we saw was the same creature; neither sea lion, seal nor sea otter, that Steller describes in some detail."

If those aboard the *Tzu Hang* really did spot the elusive Steller's sea ape, it's one of a very small number of sightings of the creature. Perhaps the animal still exists in the depths of the northern oceans.

Steller was highly reliable and cataloged a large number of species. Yet this one animal that has not been firmly identified leads some to believe he was a failed observer, a rather ridiculous assumption considering the man's track record.

It's possible that Steller spotted an animal with an already declining population, one that was wiped out in the ensuing years when waves of fur hunters poured into the region.

Whatever the sea ape was, it remains a fascinating footnote in the annals of cryptozoology.

THE RHYTINA, OR SEA-COW (Extinct)

The flesh of this animal constituted the chief food supply of Bering's shipwrecked crew, 1741-'42

Vintage engraving of Steller's Sea Cow

Steller's Sea Cow

The Sea Ape wasn't the only unusual creature Georg Steller documented during his journey.

While Steller and the crew were shipwrecked, they caught whatever they could to eat. One of the species that became a food source for the men was dubbed the "Steller's Sea Cow." A written description from 1881 described the creature:

"Steller's sea cow...was of a dark-brown color, sometimes varied with white spots or streaks. The thick leathery skin was covered with hair which grew together so as to form an exterior skin, which was full of vermin and resembled the bark of an old oak...The head was small in proportion to the large thick body, the neck short, the body diminishing rapidly behind the short fore-leg terminated abruptly without fingers or nails, but was overgrown with a number of short thickly placed brush-hairs: the hind-leg was replaced by a tail-fin resembling a whale's. The animal wanted teeth, but was instead provided with two masticating plates, one in the gum, the other in the under jaw. The udders of the female, which abounded in milk, were placed between the fore-limbs."

Much of what is known about the sea cow comes from the observations Steller made and recorded during his time stranded on the island. By Steller's account, the sea cow was a highly social animal that lived in small family groups. The animals were apparently monogamous and would routinely help injured members of their group.

Steller recounted an incident when a female was being captured. Other members of the group began ramming the hunting boat and rocking it in an attempt to rescue the endangered female. The sea cows mate even followed the boat to shore after the female had been killed. The animals lived mainly on kelp and communicated with a series of sighs and snorting sounds.

The stranded sailors survived their time on the island by hunting and eating the sea cows. Steller noted that the creature's blubber was 3-4 inches thick and tasted like almond oil. He also reported that the meat of the animal was similar to corned beef, though it was tough and needed to be cooked longer. The animal's fat was used for both cooking and as an odorless lamp oil. Additionally, the milk from females was used to make butter and as a drink.

Researchers believe the sea cow was a sirenian, related to dugongs and manatees. Sirenians are aquatic mammals with fish-like forked tails and flippers for forelimbs. The largest known living sirenian is the Caribbean manatee which can grow up to 15 feet (4.6m) in length.

Steller's sea cow was a much larger member of the species. It grew to as much as 26 to 30 feet (7.9 – 9.1m) in length. Steller himself gave two estimates of the creature's weight but scientists believe the animal's true weight was about 8-10 t (8.8-11.0 short tons/8.0 – 10.0 metric tonnes). The sea cow's large size was probably an adaption to reduce its surface area to volume ratio and conserve heat. The sea cow was especially buoyant and unable to completely submerge. It had a thick outer skin to protect it against injury from ice and sharp rocks.

Sadly, less than 30 years after Steller documented the sea cow, the animal had been hunted into extinction.

Modern researchers speculate the animal was already fading from existence by the time Steller discovered it. In the 1740s, the last remaining members of the species may have been the ones in the Bering Sea between Alaska and Russia.

The last officially confirmed sea cows were killed in 1768, but there continued to be sporadic reports of the animals well afterwards. Hunters on Bering Island claimed they took some sea cows in 1780, and accounts continued to crop up into the 1800s.

Benedykt Dybowski, a naturalist from Poland, believed the species survived as late as 1830.

In the late 1800s, Swedish naturalist Baron Erik Nordenskjold spent time on Bering Island and heard accounts of Steller's sea cow while he was there.

Two locals on Bering Island claimed a sighting of a sea cow in 1854 and they shared details with the naturalist. The men, Deodor Mertchenin and Nicanor Stepnoff, said they encountered the creature on the eastern side of the island and that it was like nothing they had ever seen before. They said the animal had brown skin, no dorsal fin and small forefeet. Furthermore, the creature's forebody was very thick and tapered off towards the back. It blew air out of its large mouth and when it did so, about fifteen feet (4.6m) of its body's length rose above the surface of the water.

Nordenskjold believed the men had encountered a Steller's sea cow, though some later researchers dispute the sighting and believe the men saw another marine animal.

Still, there continued to be occasional sightings of sea cows. Even beyond the 1800s, some believed the animals may still be alive.

Between 1910-1913, some Russian fishermen reportedly found a dead Steller's sea cow on Siberia's easternmost tip, the Cape of Chaplin. The location is close to the Bering Strait and it's believed the animal was washed in by the sea's current. Unfortunately, there was no follow up on the sighting.

Were sea cows still roaming the seas? Perhaps they moved farther from Alaskan waters and headed for remote regions. Cryptozoologist Roy P. Mackal speculated that some sea cows had avoided extinction and still survived in the wild by moving out of areas frequented by hunters.

As the 1900s rolled on, the creatures continued to be sighted in various locations.

In the early 1950s, a Russian harpooner named Ivan Skripkin said sea cows were still visiting the waters off Bering Island each July. Bering Island was a spot the creatures frequented for decades, but they may have migrated into Russian territory to survive. In July 1962, crewmen aboard the Russian whaling ship *Buran* reported six sea cows near Cape Navarin. The animals were grazing on seaweed in shallow water off Kamchatka in the Gulf of Anadyr. According to the ship's crew, the animals ranged in size from 20 to 26 feet (6.1 – 7.9m) and had trunks and split lips. The animals had small heads that were clearly delineated from the body and sharply fringed tails. The men observed the creatures from about 300 feet (91m) away. The account was published the following year in the USSR's Academy of Sciences journal.

Fishermen and locals around the northern Kuril Islands have also reported sightings of the creatures.

In the summer of 1976, salmon workers at a factory at Anapkinskaya Bay south of Cape Navarin saw and touched the carcass of a stranded sea cow. One man, Ivan Chechulin, was interviewed by a representative from the Kamchatka Museum of Local Lore. Chechulin said the animal had very dark skin, flippers and a forked tail. The creature also had a prominent snout. When shown pictures of various sea creatures, Chechulin identified the creature he saw as a Steller's sea cow.

British explorer Derek Hutchinson launched an expedition in the late 1970s, hoping to find surviving sea cows around the Aleutian Islands. His explorations yielded no results. Likewise, the search conducted by Soviet scientist Dr. Anatoly Shkunkov conducted in the 1980s off Kamchatka came up empty.

For years, even skeletal remains of the animals were scarce. In the 19th century, bones of sea cows were in demand, and, when found, were usually sold to museums at high prices.

In November 2017, researchers from the Commander Islands Nature and Biosphere Reserve found a skeleton of a Steller's sea cow. The skeleton consisted of 45 spinal bones, 27 ribs, a left shoulder blade, shoulder and forearm bones and several wrist bones. The skeleton was found during regular monitoring of the coastal line Marina Shitova.

Ultimately, the story of the Steller's sea cow is a sad one. A gentle animal wiped from existence. The slow moving and docile animals were easy targets for hunters who wanted if for its meat, fat and hide. The creatures were hunted far more quickly than they could reproduce.

But, like other cryptids, there remains the possibility that they still dwell somewhere in the depths, well away from humans. Time, and exploration, may again lead to their discovery.

Steller's Sea Raven

There's another mysterious animal reported by Steller from his time being shipwrecked on Bering Island. He referred to the creature as a "white sea-raven" and said it was a "rare bird." Reportedly the bird was "...not seen in the Siberian coast."

Dubbed the "Steller's Sea Raven," the naturalist wrote that the bird was a cliff dweller and so was impossible to reach. He wrote that the bird resembled a cormorant.

Researchers have looked at possible known birds that fit Steller's description of the Sea Raven. Candidates include the pigeon guillemot with a white, winter plumage and a species of Pacific sandpiper called the surf bird.

Danish Cryptozoologist Lars Thomas from Copenhagen's Zoological Museum made an interesting point about the sea raven mystery when he noted that Germans refer to cormorants as sea ravens. Since Steller was German, it's very likely he was indeed describing a cormorant, one that may now be extinct, such as the spectacled cormorant.

In a dialogue with cryptozoologist Karl Shuker, Thomas further argued that Steller's mention of a white sea raven may actually refer to either an albino or young specimen of white cormorant.

Researcher Chris Orrick has closely studied Steller's publications and related works. He told Shuker that in a letter from Steller to the Russian Academy, the naturalist stated that he had prepared a paper on Bering Island's birds and fishes. It's possible the paper contains further details on the mysterious sea raven but sadly, the document has not been found so far.

Orrick himself speculates that the sea raven may be a species that is currently known to science but was unknown during Steller's time. He suggests the surfbird, a white-plumed bird native to Alaska and the Pacific coast as a possible candidate.

The sea raven presents an interesting puzzle. No other accounts of the bird have surfaced and truthfully, we may never know its identity. It's possible the bird was misidentified or is more commonly known by a different name, or it could be a long extinct species.

Steller's lost manuscript may still be in the Academy archives in St. Petersburg, so hopefully, it will turn up at some point and offer more clues to the mystery of the Steller's sea raven.

Bibliography

Abercrombie, W.R.B. Alaska 1899 Copper River Exploring Expedition. Captain W.R. Abercrombie, Second U.S. Infantry, Commanding. Washington, Government Printing Office, Washington, D.C. 1900.

Alley, Robert J. Raincoast Sasquatch. Hancock House Publishers Surrey, B.C./Blaine, WA. 2003.

Barazzuol, Richard. The Tlingit Land Otter Complex: Coherence in the Social and Shamanic Order independent paper. 1981.

Beck, Mary Giraudo. Shamans and Kushtakas North Coast Tales of the Supernatural. Alaska Northwest Books, Bothell, WA 1991.

Christopher, Neil, and Austin, Mike. The Hidden. Inhabit Media Inc., Toronto, Ontario, 2014.

Cobb, Norma, and Sasser, Charles W. Artic Homestead: The True Story of One Family's Survival and Courage in the Alaskan Wilds. St. Martin's Griffin, New York, NY 2003.

Coleman, Loren and Huyghe, Patrick. The Field Guide to Lake Monsters, Sea Serpents, and other Mystery Denizens of the Deep. Tarcher/Penguin, New York, NY. 2003.

Colp, Harry D. The Strangest Story Ever Told. Exposition Press, New York, NY 1953.

Dihle, Bjorn. Haunted Inside Passage Ghosts, Legends, and Mysteries of Southeast Alaska. Alaska Northwest Books, Portland, OR, 2017.

Ellis-Knapp, Jody. Ghosts of Alaska, Schiffer Publishing Ltd., Atglen, PA, 2009.

Emmons, George Thornton, de Laguna, Frederica editor.

The Tlingit Indians. University of Washington Press, Seattle, WA. 1991.

Gerhard, Ken. A Menagerie of Mysterious Beasts. Llewellyn Publications, Woodbury, Minn. 2016.

Green, John Sasquatch the Apes Among Us. Hancock House Publishers Surrey, B.C./Blaine, WA. 2006.

Hall, Mark A. Thunderbirds America's Living Legends of Giant Birds. Paraview Press, New York, NY 2004.

Halliday, Jan. Native Peoples of Alaska. Sasquatch Books, Seattle, WA 1998.

Heuvelmans, Bernard. In The Wake of Sea Serpents. Hill & Wang Publishing, New York, NY 1969.

Kirk, John, In the Domain of Lake Monsters. Key Porter Books Limited, Toronto, Ontario 1998.

LeBlond, Paul and Bousfield, Edward. Cadborosaurus: Survivor From the Deep. Heritage House 2000.

Mackal, Roy. Searching For Hidden Animals An Inquiry into Zoological Mysteries. Doubleday & Company, Inc., Garden City, NY, 1980.

McCorkle, Ruth and Walluk, Wilbur. Alaskan Ten Footed Bear and other legends. Coachwhip Publications, Greenville, OH 2013.

Nelson, Richard K. Make Prayers to the Raven A Koyukon View of the Northern Forest. University of Chicago Press, Chicago, IL 1983.

Place, Martin. Bigfoot All Over the Country. Dodd Mead Publishing, New York, NY 1978.

Redfern, Nick, The Bigfoot Book The Encyclopedia of Sasquatch, Yeti and Cryptid Primates. Visible Ink Press, Canton, MI. 2016.

Sherwonit, Bill, Living with Wildness: An Alaskan Odyssey. University of Alaska Press, College, AK 2008.

Smeeton, Miles, The Misty Islands. Nautical Publishing Company, Captain's Row, Lymington, Hampshire, UK 1969.

Steller, Georg, Journal of a Voyage with Bering, 1741-1742. Stanford University Press, Palo Alto, CA 1993.

Swanton, John Reed. Tlingit Myths and Texts, Recorded by John R. Swanton. Smithsonian Institution Bureau of American Ethnology Bulletin 39, Washington, D.C. 1909.

Wade, Jeremy. River Monsters True Stories of the Ones that Didn't Get Away. Da Capo Press, Philadelphia, PA, 2011.

Wendt, Ron. Haunted Alaska Ghost Stories from the Far North. Epicenter Press, Kenmore, WA, 2002.

Zantua, Kanoe. Princess Island Legends. Self-published, Ketchikan, AK 1997.

Websites

http://bfro.net

https://cryptomundo.com

http://www.cryptozoonews.com

The Author in Alaska

About the Author

David Weatherly is a renaissance man of the strange and supernatural. He has traveled the world in pursuit of ghosts, cryptids, UFOs, magic, and more. From the specters of dusty castles, to remote, haunted islands, from ancient sites, to modern mysteries, he has journeyed to the most unusual places on the globe seeking the unknown.

David became fascinated with the paranormal at a young age. Ghost stories and accounts of weird creatures and UFOs led him to discover many of his early influences. Writers such as John Keel, Jacques Vallee, Hans Holzer and others set him on course to spend his life exploring and investigating the unexplained.

Throughout his life, he's also delved into shamanic and magical traditions from around the world, spending time with elders from numerous cultures in Europe, the Americas, Africa and Asia. He has studied with Taoist masters in China, Tibetan Lamas, and other mystics from the Far East. He's picked up knowledge from African and Native American tribal elders and sat around fires with shamans from countless other traditions.

Along his path, David has also gathered a lot of arcane knowledge, studying a range of ancient arts from palmistry, the runes, and other obscure forms of divination, including alchemy and magick. He has studied and taught Qigong and Ninjutsu, as well as various energy-related arts. David has also studied stage and performance magic.

His shamanic and magical background has given him a unique perspective in his explorations into the unknown, and he continues to write, travel and explore, leaving no stone unturned in his quest for the strange and unusual.

David has investigated and written about a diverse range of topics including, Hauntings & Ghosts, Cryptozoology, Ufology, Ancient Mysteries, Shamanism, Magic and Psychic Phenomena.

In 2012, David founded an independent media and publishing company.

He has been a featured speaker at conferences around the world and has lectured for countless paranormal and spiritual groups.

He is a frequent guest on Coast to Coast AM with George Noory, Spaced Out Radio and other radio programs. David has also appeared on numerous television shows including the Travel Channel's Mysteries of the Outdoors, History Channel's Ancient Aliens, Beyond Belief and other programs.

David's books include *Strange Intruders*, *Black Eyed Children* the *Wood Knocks* series, and the Monsters of America series.

To find David online

https://eerielights.com/